Success

Assessment Papers

KS3 Maths

LEVELS
6-7

Bob Hartman

Sample page

paper number for
quick reference

level showing
attainment target

non-calculator
symbol

integrated mark
scheme

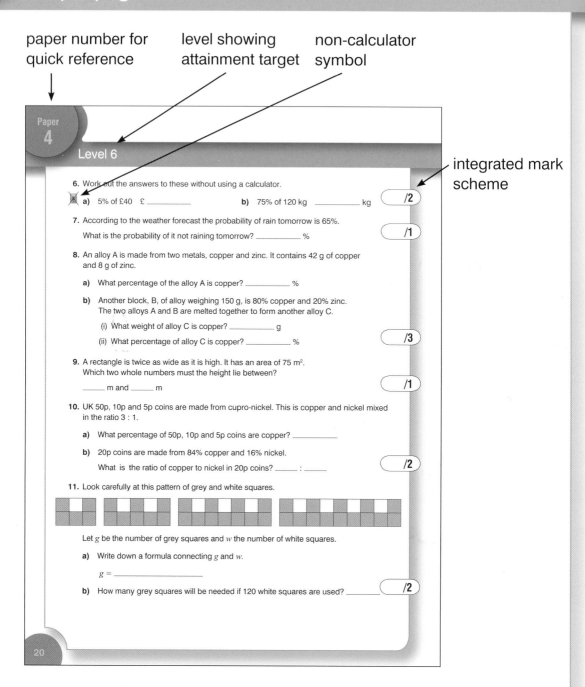

Paper 4

Level 6

6. Work out the answers to these without using a calculator.

   a) 5% of £40   £ _____   b)   75% of 120 kg _____ kg   /2

7. According to the weather forecast the probability of rain tomorrow is 65%.

   What is the probability of it not raining tomorrow? _____ %   /1

8. An alloy A is made from two metals, copper and zinc. It contains 42 g of copper and 8 g of zinc.

   a)   What percentage of the alloy A is copper? _____ %

   b)   Another block, B, of alloy weighing 150 g, is 80% copper and 20% zinc.
        The two alloys A and B are melted together to form another alloy C.

       (i) What weight of alloy C is copper? _____ g

       (ii) What percentage of alloy C is copper? _____ %   /3

9. A rectangle is twice as wide as it is high. It has an area of 75 m².
   Which two whole numbers must the height lie between?

   _____ m and _____ m   /1

10. UK 50p, 10p and 5p coins are made from cupro-nickel. This is copper and nickel mixed in the ratio 3 : 1.

    a)   What percentage of 50p, 10p and 5p coins are copper? _____

    b)   20p coins are made from 84% copper and 16% nickel.

         What is the ratio of copper to nickel in 20p coins? _____ : _____   /2

11. Look carefully at this pattern of grey and white squares.

    Let g be the number of grey squares and w the number of white squares.

    a)   Write down a formula connecting g and w.

         $g =$ _____

    b)   How many grey squares will be needed if 120 white squares are used? _____   /2

20

2

Contents

PAPER 1	4
PAPER 2	9
PAPER 3	14
PAPER 4	18
PAPER 5	23
PAPER 6	28
PAPER 7	31
PAPER 8	35
PAPER 9	39
PAPER 10	43
PAPER 11	47
PAPER 12	52
PAPER 13	55
PAPER 14	60
PAPER 15	63
PAPER 16	67
PAPER 17	70
PAPER 18	74
Glossary	78
Progress grid	80
Answer booklet	1–8

PAPER 1

1. On a separate sheet of squared paper draw a grid with x and y axes both extending from −5 to 10.
The lines $y = 2x$, $x = 1$ and $y = x + 4$, form a triangle. Write down the vertices of the triangle.

(_____ , _____) (_____ , _____) (_____ , _____)

/3

2. Which of these gives the cheapest netbook computer and by how much?
Buy Best   20% off original price of £213
Bestest Buy   15% off original price of £195
Cheap cheep   12% off original price of £176

_____ is the cheapest by £ _____

/2

3. Write these shapes in order of their area, smallest area first.

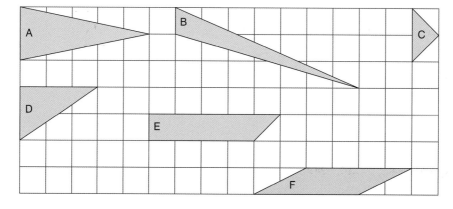

_____

/1

4. a) Write the following information as an equation, where x is the larger of the two numbers.
"Three times the larger of two consecutive even numbers is 20 more than the sum of the two numbers."

_____

b) Solve your equation to find the two numbers. _____ and _____

/2

5. How far does the tip of the second hand of a watch travel each day if its radius is 1 cm?
(Take $\pi = 3.1$) _____ m

/2

6.

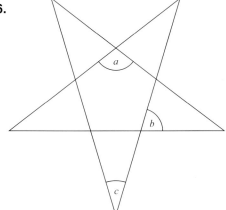

This star is made from a regular pentagon.
Find the sizes of the angles marked with letters.

$a =$ _____ °

$b =$ _____ °

$c =$ _____ °

/3

7. Amy wants to see if heavier books have more pages. She weighs 10 books and notes the number of pages in each. Her results are shown in this table.

Number of pages	116	156	96	96	132	132	140	124	132	84
Weight (g)	230	330	200	180	320	260	290	260	350	160

a) Plot these results on the scatter graph.

b) What does your scatter graph show about weights of books and the number of pages they have?

_____

_____

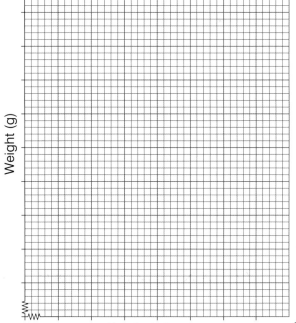

Weight (g)

Number of pages

/2

8. Find the area of this ring.
   (Take π = 3.1)

   [handwritten:]
   6 17
   ~~78.15~~ cm² (1dp)
   - 49.6 cm²
   28.9 cm²

   2 8 . 9 cm²

   $A = π × r^2 =$ $π × 4cm^2 = 49.6cm²$

   Beark
   $π × 5cm^2 = 465$ 78.54cm² (2dp)

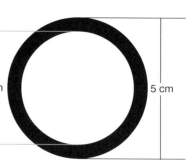

24 cm

5 cm

/2

9. Triangle A is mapped onto triangle B.

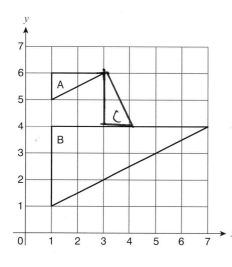

a) Describe fully the transformation that does this.

   [handwritten:] It enlarges by the scale factor 3

b) What remains unchanged when A is transformed into B?

   [handwritten:] The shape and the side it's on

c) Draw the image of A after it has been transformed by a rotation of 90° anti-clockwise about the point (3, 6).

d) What remains unchanged after this transformation?

   [handwritten:] The size ~~and~~ of the shape

/5

10. According to the Royal Mail, 93% of first class letters should arrive the next working day and 98.5% of second class letters should arrive within three working days after posting. Using these figures, what is the probability of a first class letter not arriving the next day?

    Give your answer as a decimal. *[handwritten:]* 0.07

/1

11. Jan has two counters, one white the other black.
    Each counter has a cross on one side and a tick on the other.

a) List all the possible outcomes when she flips the two counters, for example:
   What is the total number of outcomes?

   [handwritten:] ✓x , xx , x✓ , ✓✓   ~~so~~ there are 4 possible outcomes.

b) What is the probability that both counters show the same symbol?

   [handwritten:] 50%

/2

12. Here are some nets. Some of them fold up to make an open-topped cube. Circle the letters of the nets that fold to make open-topped cubes.

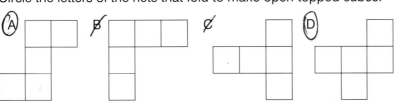

/1

13. Here is a two-way table showing the results of a survey into cars that were over 10 years old and whether or not they were red.

	10 or more years old	Not 10 or more years old	Total
Red	20	50	70
Not red	60	300	360
Total	80	350	380 430

a) How many cars were surveyed? _____ 430

b) How many cars that were 10 or more years old were found? _____ 80

c) How many 10 or more year-old cars were not red? _____ 60

/3

14. Look at this sequence of numbers:

4   10   22   46   9.4

The rule to generate each number from the number before it is:

"Add 1 and then multiply by two."

a) Write the next two numbers in the sequence. _____ 94 _____ 190

b) Fill in the missing terms of this sequence. It uses the same rule but a different first term.

_____ 3 _____ 8 _____ 18   38   78   158

/3

15. An ironing board rests on two legs of equal length.
The board and floor are both horizontal.

Calculate the sizes of angles a, b and c.
Give a reason for each answer,
(e.g. "*Alternate angles*").

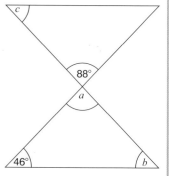

$a = $ __88__ ° because *its horizonty oppisite to 88°*
$b = $ __134__ ° because *Of three angles in a triangle*
$c = $ __134__ ° because *crossxtionaily oppisite*

/3

16. What is the sum of the internal angles of this polygon?

__5a__ °

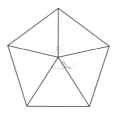

/1

17. Solve this puzzle which originated in Ancient Greece two thousand years ago.

"What number must be added to 100 and 20 – the same to
both – so that the answers are in the ratio 3 : 1?"

__160__

/1

18. Find the missing fractions to make these calculations correct.
Write them in their simplest form.

a) $\dfrac{3}{5} + \boxed{\dfrac{25}{30}} = \dfrac{28}{35}$ b) $\boxed{\dfrac{12}{24}} - \dfrac{1}{4} = \dfrac{11}{20}$ c) $3 \times \dfrac{2}{9} = \boxed{\dfrac{6}{27}}$

/3

/40

PAPER 2

1. Find angles a and b in this diagram of a kite.

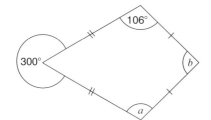

$a = $ _____ °

$b = $ _____ °

/2

2. Each side of this octagon measures 1 cm.

a) What is the perimeter of a line of three octagons like these?

_____ cm

b) What is the perimeter of a line of n octagons? _____

/2

3. What is the least number of colours needed to paint the faces of a cube so that no two faces next to each other are coloured the same?

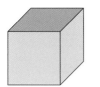

_____

/1

4.

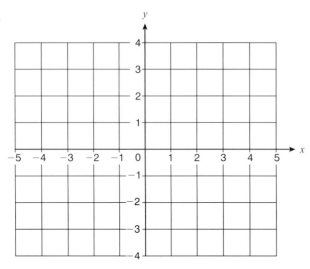

a) Draw the straight line $y = x$

b) Draw the straight line $y = x + 2$

c) Draw a reflection of the line $y = x + 2$ in the line $y = x$.
Write down the equation of this straight line.

_____

/3

5. A rug is in the shape of a semi-circle with radius 90 cm. What is its area to the nearest 0.1 m²?

(Take $\pi = 3.1$) _____ m²

/1

6. When you sell something at auction you have to pay the auctioneers. This is called commission and is usually a percentage of the price that the item is sold for. The internet auction house, Ezeesell, charges a commission on a sliding scale. Up to £29.99, it is 5.25% of the winning bid. From £30.00 to £599.99, it is 5.25% of the first £29.99, then 3.25% of the balance.

Jan sells her mountain bike on Ezeesell for £50.

How much commission will she have to pay?   £ _____

/2

7. A drugs company is testing a new spot cream. It is comparing the new cream with its old one. The number of people whose spots were cured was found for each cream. The results are shown in this partly complete two-way table.

	Old cream	New cream	Total
Cured	600	450	
Not cured	200	150	
Total			

a) Complete the table.

b) How many people took part in the test? _____

c) How many people using the new cream were cured? _____

d) What proportion of people were cured using:

(i) the new cream _____%

(ii) the old cream _____%

e) Which cream was more effective, the old or the new, and why?

_____ because _____

/6

8. I think of a number, square it, and add half the original number. The answer is 203.

What number was I first thinking of? _____

/1

9. Solve these equations.

a) $5(3x + 1) = 35$ $x =$ _____

b) $2 + 5x = 10 - 3x$ $x =$ _____

c) $2(x + 1) = x + 5$ $x =$ _____

/3

10. Aijaz has a fair triangular and a fair square spinner. In a game he spins both spinners and adds together the numbers on each. This gives the score.

	Square spinner			
	1	2	3	4
1				
2				
3				

Triangular spinner

a) Complete this table showing all the possible scores.

b) How many different scores are possible? _____

c) What is the probability of not getting a score of 2? _____

/3

11

11. A piece of wire is bent into the shape of a right-angled triangle with sides of length 37 cm, 35 cm and 12 cm.

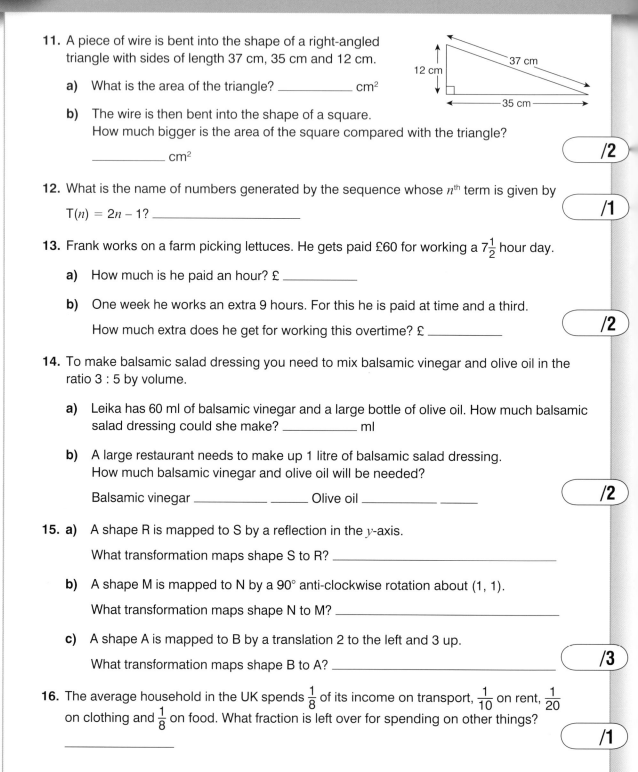

a) What is the area of the triangle? _____ cm²

b) The wire is then bent into the shape of a square. How much bigger is the area of the square compared with the triangle?

_____ cm²

/2

12. What is the name of numbers generated by the sequence whose n^{th} term is given by $T(n) = 2n - 1$? _____

/1

13. Frank works on a farm picking lettuces. He gets paid £60 for working a $7\frac{1}{2}$ hour day.

a) How much is he paid an hour? £ _____

b) One week he works an extra 9 hours. For this he is paid at time and a third.

How much extra does he get for working this overtime? £ _____

/2

14. To make balsamic salad dressing you need to mix balsamic vinegar and olive oil in the ratio 3 : 5 by volume.

a) Leika has 60 ml of balsamic vinegar and a large bottle of olive oil. How much balsamic salad dressing could she make? _____ ml

b) A large restaurant needs to make up 1 litre of balsamic salad dressing. How much balsamic vinegar and olive oil will be needed?

Balsamic vinegar _____ _____ Olive oil _____ _____

/2

15. a) A shape R is mapped to S by a reflection in the y-axis.

What transformation maps shape S to R? _____

b) A shape M is mapped to N by a 90° anti-clockwise rotation about (1, 1).

What transformation maps shape N to M? _____

c) A shape A is mapped to B by a translation 2 to the left and 3 up.

What transformation maps shape B to A? _____

/3

16. The average household in the UK spends $\frac{1}{8}$ of its income on transport, $\frac{1}{10}$ on rent, $\frac{1}{20}$ on clothing and $\frac{1}{8}$ on food. What fraction is left over for spending on other things?

_____

/1

17. Mark starts to take a bath. After 3 minutes there are 30 litres of water in the bath. He then turns the water-flow down, taking 3 minutes to add 10 litres. He finishes filling the bath by adding another 10 litres which takes a minute. Mark takes 4 minutes to have his bath, then lets the water out which takes two minutes.

Show this "story" on the grid.
(Assume that the water flows in and empties steadily.)

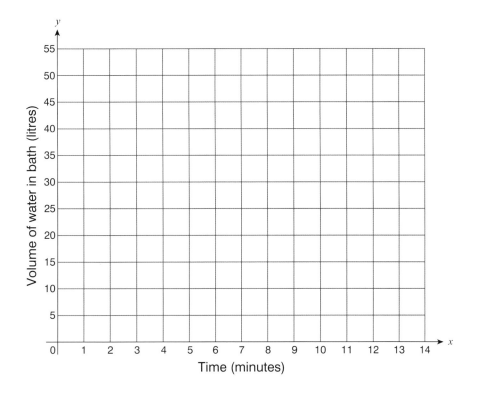

/2

18. A cuboid is made from 1 centimetre cubes. It has a volume of 24 cm².

a) What are the possible dimensions of the cuboid?

_____

b) The cuboid has a total surface area of 56 cm². What are the dimensions of the cuboid?

_____ cm by _____ cm by _____ cm

/3

/40

PAPER 3

1. Asif spends his free time one Saturday evening as follows:

- 5 hours on the internet
- 2 hours on his games console
- 1 hour chatting on his mobile phone

a) What **fraction** of his time was spent on the internet? _____

b) What **percentage** of his time was spent on his games console? _____

/2

2. Find general terms for each of the following sequences, for example:

8, 10, 12, 14,... General term is   ___2n + 6___

a) 5, 14, 23, 32,... General term is _____

b) 4, 5, 6, 7, 8,... General term is _____

c) 3, 6, 9, 12,... General term is _____

/3

3. You are given that $5p - 3q = 14$.

a) Find p when $q = 2$ $p =$ _____

b) Find q when $p = -5$ $q =$ _____

/2

4. Find the missing angles in this diagram.

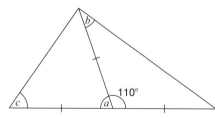

$a =$ _____ °

$b =$ _____ °

$c =$ _____ °

/3

5. Alice spins a spinner, numbered from 1 to 4.

a) Complete the table below to show the probability that she obtains a 3.

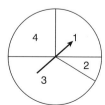

Number	1	2	3	4
Probability	0.25	0.125	_____	0.25

b) If Alice spins the spinner 100 times, how many times should she expect

to spin a 4? _____

6. The weights (in kg) of 20 teenagers are as follows.

| 123.5 | 119.9 | 146.0 | 127.1 | 120.1 | 135.6 | 138.0 | 130.1 | 118.2 | 110.5 |
| 130.2 | 126.6 | 119.8 | 132.3 | 130.0 | 142.0 | 126.0 | 110.0 | 119.0 | 140.0 |

Complete this grouped frequency table.

Weight (w kg)	Frequency
$110 \le w < 120$	
$120 \le w < 130$	
$130 \le w < 140$	
$140 \le w < 150$	

7. A cobbled path is to be constructed around a circular pond. The diameter of the outside of the path is 50 m and the diameter of the pond is 30 m.

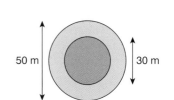

50 m   30 m

a) Find the area of the pond (to 3 s.f.). Use the value of π on your calculator.

Area _____ _____

b) To cobble the path costs £45 per square metre of path.

How much to the nearest £10 will the cobbled path cost? £ _____

8. Find the missing angles in the following diagram.

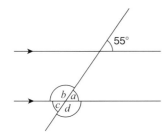

55°

b a
c d

$a =$ _____ °

$b =$ _____ °

$c =$ _____ °

$d =$ _____ °

9. Work out the answers to the following.

a) $\frac{1}{2} + \frac{1}{7} =$ _____

b) $\frac{1}{3} - \frac{1}{4} =$ _____

c) $\frac{1}{2} + \frac{1}{3} + \frac{1}{4} =$ _____

/3

10. A cube has each side equal to x cm.
If $x = 1$, the total surface area is 6 cm² while the volume is 1 cm³.
Similarly, if $x = 10$ the total surface area is 600 cm² while the volume is 1000 cm³.

a) Write an equation given that the surface area and volume of a cube, side x cm,

have the same numerical value. _____

b) For what value of x will the total surface area and the volume actually have the

same numerical value? $x =$ _____ cm

/2

11. The following pie chart shows the destinations of 90 people selected at random at
Heathrow airport one Saturday morning. Calculate the angles marked p, q and r.

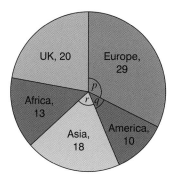

$p =$ _____ °

$q =$ _____ °

$r =$ _____ °

/3

12. Find the area (to 3 s.f.) of the shaded part of this quarter-circle.

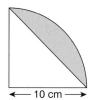

Area = _____ cm²

/2

13. Describe the correlation in each of the following scatter diagrams.

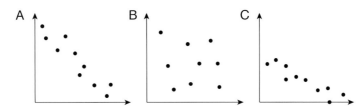

    a) A is an example of _____ correlation.

    b) B is an example of _____ correlation.

    c) C is an example of _____ correlation.

/3

14. Sammy the Siamese cat always eats fish for her lunch, with a choice of salmon, shrimps or tuna.

The probability that she eats shrimps is twice the probability that she eats salmon.

The probability that she eats tuna is three times the probability that she eats salmon.

Write down (as a fraction) the probability that she eats:

    a) salmon _____

    b) shrimps _____

    c) tuna   _____

/3

/40

PAPER 4

1. Solve these equations.

    a) $x + 4 = 12$ $\qquad$ $x =$ _____

    b) $2x + 3 = 17$ $\qquad$ $x =$ _____

    c) $14x - 99 = 5x$ $\qquad$ $x =$ _____

    d) $7x - 4 = 4x + 8$ $\quad$ $x =$ _____

    /4

2. Complete this magic square involving fractions.
   Write the fractions in their simplest terms.
   (In a magic square the numbers in each column,
   row and diagonal have the same total.)

	$\frac{1}{8}$	$\frac{5}{8}$
$\frac{3}{8}$	$\frac{1}{2}$	
	$\frac{7}{8}$	$\frac{1}{4}$

    /3

3. Work out the sizes of the angles marked with letters.
   In each case give a reason.

    $a =$ _____° because _____

    $b =$ _____° because _____

    $c =$ _____° because _____

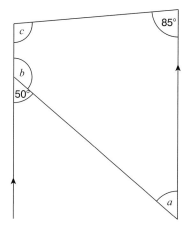

    /3

4. A market gardener is experimenting growing two types of apple tree.
One is called Freyberg, the other Malster. She picks the same number of apples from each tree and weighs them. Here are her results on two frequency charts.

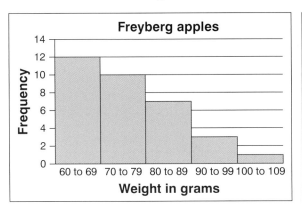

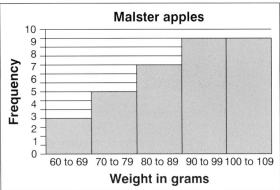

a) How many Freyberg apples did she pick? _____

b) How many of the Malster apples were less than 80 g? _____

c) Which type gives the bigger apples?

_____ because _____

/3

5. Jennifer is playing this game with her friend Anita. Jennifer is "odd" and Anita "even". They throw two 6-sided dice and take the difference of the two numbers showing. If this is odd Jennifer wins, if it is even Anita wins. If the difference is zero neither of them win and the dice are thrown again.

a) Complete this table showing all the possible results.

		Number on the other dice					
		1	2	3	4	5	6
Number on one dice	1	0	1	2	3	4	5
	2	1	0	1	2	3	4
	3	2	1	0	1	2	3
	4	3	2	1	0	1	2
	5						
	6						

b) What is the probability of Jennifer winning a game? _____

c) Is the game a fair game? _____ because _____

/3

6. Work out the answers to these without using a calculator.

a) 5% of £40 £ _____

b) 75% of 120 kg _____ kg

/2

7. According to the weather forecast the probability of rain tomorrow is 65%.

What is the probability of it not raining tomorrow? _____ %

/1

8. An alloy A is made from two metals, copper and zinc. It contains 42 g of copper and 8 g of zinc.

a) What percentage of alloy A is copper? _____ %

b) Another block, B, of alloy weighing 150 g, is 80% copper and 20% zinc. The two alloys A and B are melted together to form another alloy, C.

(i) What weight of alloy C is copper? _____ g

(ii) What percentage of alloy C is copper? _____ %

/3

9. A rectangle is twice as wide as it is high. It has an area of 75 m². Which two whole numbers must the height lie between?

_____ m and _____ m

/1

10. UK 50p, 10p and 5p coins are made from cupro-nickel. This is copper and nickel mixed in the ratio 3 : 1.

a) What percentage of 50p, 10p and 5p coins are copper? _____

b) 20p coins are made from 84% copper and 16% nickel.

What is the ratio of copper to nickel in 20p coins? _____ : _____

/2

11. Look carefully at this pattern of grey and white squares.

Let g be the number of grey squares and w the number of white squares.

a) Write down a formula connecting g and w.

g = _____

b) How many grey squares will be needed if 120 white squares are used? _____

/2

12. Here are two solids made from cubes.

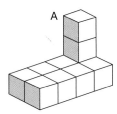

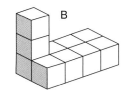

Match A or B with each of these drawings.

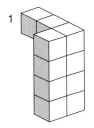 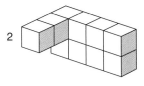 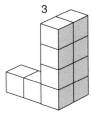

1 = _____   2 = _____

3 = _____   4 = _____

5 = _____   6 = _____

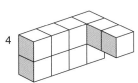 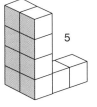 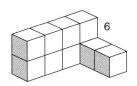

/2

13. A cuboid is made from 1 cm cubes. It has a volume of 36 cm³.
What are the possible dimensions of the cuboid? Give three different sized cuboids.

_____ by _____ by _____   OR   _____ by _____ by _____   OR   _____ by _____ by _____

/1

14. Here are three commands for moving a model turtle.

> FD 4 means move forwards 4 units, RT 45 means turn 45° clockwise and
> LT 90 means turn 90° anti-clockwise.

On a separate sheet of squared paper, starting from point P, facing up the page, show the
path drawn by these commands.

FD 1	RT 90	FD 1	LT 90	FD 2	RT 90	FD 1
RT 90	FD 3	RT 90	FD 2			

/1

15. The Royal Albert Hall, in London, is a circular building of diameter 100 m.

   a) How far is it to walk once round the outside of the Albert Hall? _____ m

   b) How many times would you need to walk round to cover 1 km? _____

   c) What is the ground area taken up by the Albert Hall? _____ m²

/3

16. Safia is about to draw a pie chart showing the proportion of people of different ages in the UK.

   a) Complete her table below.

Age (years)	Percentage	Angle (nearest whole number)
0 to 14	17	61°
15 to 64	67	_____°
65+	16	_____°

   b) On a separate piece of paper, draw and label Safia's completed pie chart.

/2

17. Match each straight line to one of the equations in the box.

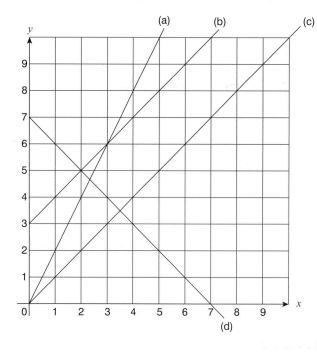

[1] $y = x$	[2] $y = x + 3$
[3] $y = 3x$	[4] $x = 3y$
[5] $y = 2x$	[6] $y = x + 4$
[7] $y = x - 7$	[8] $y = 7 - x$

a) _____

b) _____

c) _____

d) _____

/4

/40

PAPER 5

1. a) Complete this table which shows all the possible outcomes when a fair 6-sided dice and a fair coin are tossed at the same time.

		Score on dice					
		1	2	3	4	5	6
Coin	Head (H)	H1	H2	H3	H4	H5	H6
	Tail (T)	T1	T2	T3	T4	T5	T6

b) What is the probability of getting:

(i) a head and a six? __1/12__

(ii) A tail and an odd number? __1/4__

/3

2. Calculate the volume of cement required to make these three garden steps. All three steps are the same size.

1n×20m = 20m²
20m²×30m
600m³

CSA
V = CSA × Length
1m×10m = 10m² × 30m
300m³

1m × 30m = 30m²
30m² × 30m = 900m³

30cm
10cm
1m

300m³
600m³
900m³
1800m³

__1800m³__

/2

3. This is an arrowhead.

100° ÷ 2 = 50°

100°C + 50°C =
150°C

360°C − 160°C =
200°C ÷ 2 =
100°C

because =
180°C − 150°C =
30°C

Calculate the size of the angle x. __30°__ °

/1

4. The London Eye wheel in London has a diameter of 135 m. There are 32 pods spaced equally round the circumference.

About how far apart along the circumference are the pods? __424.1__ m (1dp)

C = π × d =
π × 135m =

/1

5. The probability of winning any prize in the National Lottery is about 0.0185.

What is the probability of not winning a prize in the National Lottery? _0.9815_

$1 - 0.0185 =$

6. The perimeter of this triangle is 2**3** cm.

a) Write an equation in terms of x.

_4X + 3 = 23 cm_

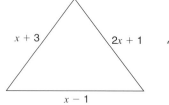

$x + 3$ $2x + 1$ $x - 1$

$4x + 3 = 25$ cm
$- 3$ cm $= - 3$ cm
$4x = 22$ cm
$\frac{4x}{4}$ $\frac{22}{4}$
$x = 5.5$

b) Solve your equation and find the lengths of all the sides of the triangle.

_8.5_ cm _4.5_ cm _12_ cm

$2 \times 5.5 + 1 =$

S.5+3 = 5.5
S. Simplar 4.5cm

$$/3$$

7. The children in a Y4 primary school class have their heights measured.
These are the results; all the heights are in centimetres.

136	109	135	126	132	122	113	126	132	127	110
118	130	141	124	138	138	127	125	109	114	140
126	128	117	138	114	124	142	150	121	136	111

a) Complete this tally table. (You may not need to use all the rows.)

Height in cm	Tally	Frequency
100 to 109	||	2
109 to 118	₩ ||	7
119 to 127	₩ |||	8
128 to 136	₩ ₩ ₩ |	6
137 to 145	₩ 1	6
146 to 150	|	1

$$/3$$

b) How many children have heights from 120 cm to 139 cm? _17_

8. Use trial and improvement to find n if $n \times (n + 6) = 342$, (n is a positive number).

Give your answer correct to 1 decimal place. _15.7_

$$/2$$

$n \mid n \times (n+6) = 342$
$3 \mid 3 \times (3+6) = 3\alpha$ too low
$8 \mid 8 \times (8+6) = 112$ too low
$24 \mid 24 \times (24+6) = 720$ too high
$12 \mid 12 \times (12+6) = 216$ too low
$18 \mid 18 \times (18+6) = 432$ too low

$16 (16 \times (16+6) = 3$
$15 (15 \times (15+6)$
$15.5 (15 \times (15.5+6) = 333$

9. This stack contains seven cubes, each of side 2 cm.
   On one centimetre squared paper, draw full size, the view looking along:

   a) A

   b) B

   c) C

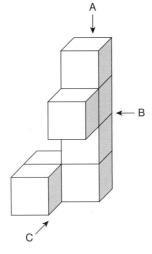

/3

10. Complete this table. The names of the quadrilaterals can be chosen from this list:

square, parallelogram, rhombus, kite and trapezium

Quadrilateral	Diagonals **always** cut at right angles	Number of lines of symmetry	Order of rotational symmetry
Rectangle	Yes	2	2
Square	Yes	4	4
Kite	Yes	1	1
Parralelagram Trapezium	Yes	0	2
Trapezium	Yes	1	2

/4

11. Here are four fraction cards.

    Put the cards into two piles which have the same total.

    3/8, 3/4   1/8, 1/2

/1

12. Two friends are arguing about CO_2 pollution from cars.
Simian says that low polluting cars use expensive exhaust systems and are more expensive than "dirty" cars. His friend Amy collects some information about the CO_2 emission (grams of CO_2 per km driven) and cost of car (in thousands of pounds). She plots this scatter graph.

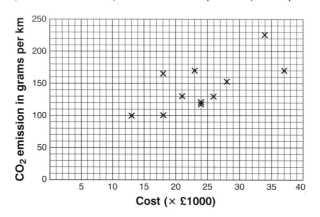

Does Amy's scatter graph support what Simian thinks?

_____ because _____

/1

13. Write these numbers in order, smallest first.

0.5 $\frac{15}{20}$ 5%   15% $\frac{1}{5}$ 0.015

_____

/1

14. Some Y9 students were asked to opt for either swimming or volley ball.
This table shows how boys and girls chose. (Give your answers to the nearest 1%.)

a) What percentage of the students were girls?

_____

b) What percentage of girls chose volley ball?

_____

	Swimming	Volley ball
Girls	33	27
Boys	28	42

/3

c) What percentage of students chose swimming? _____

15. Each side of this pentagon measures 1 cm.
A pattern is made by adding pentagons one at a time.

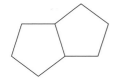

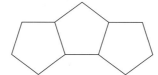

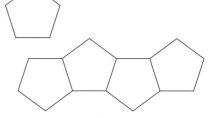

What is the perimeter of a line of:

a) 5 pentagons? _____   **b)** 10 pentagons? _____

c) n pentagons? _____   /3

16. Which of the straight lines, if any, whose equations are given in the box below, pass through the points (1,5) **and** (2,4)?

(1) $y = 2x$ (2) $y = 2x + 3$ (3) $y = x + 4$ (4) $y = 6 - x$ (5) $y = 4x + 1$ (6) $y = x$

_____   /1

17. The "gold" Euro coins are made from Nordic gold.
Nordic gold does not contain any gold! It is made from copper, aluminium, zinc and tin.
A 7.8 g 50 cent coin contains 0.39 g of copper.

What percentage of a 50 cent Euro coin is copper? _____%   /1

18. The UK £1 coin is 70% copper, 5.55% nickel and 24.5% zinc.
Angus has to show this information on a pie chart.
What angles should he use for each metal? Round your answers to the nearest degree.

Copper _____°   Nickel _____°   Zinc _____°   /2

19. Here are two commands for moving a model turtle.

FD 5 means move forwards 5 units

RT 60 means turn 60° clockwise.

Complete this list of commands to move the turtle from A to B, taking this route.
The turtle starts at facing up the page.

FD 1   RT 90   FD 2

_____   /2

20. A box weighs a grams. It contains b nuts each weighing 10 grams.

Write an expression for the total weight of the box and the nuts. _____   /1

21. How many seconds are there in 1.2 minutes? _____ seconds   /1

/40

PAPER 6

1. The nth term of a sequence is given by $5n - 2$

   a) Write down the first three terms in this sequence. _____, _____, _____

   b) For which term number will the sequence first become greater than 100? _____

                                                        /3

2. Find the perimeter (to 3 s.f.) of this semicircular shape.

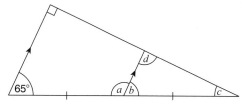

Perimeter = _____ cm

/2

3. Find the missing angles in the following diagram:

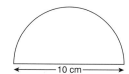

$a =$ _____ °

$b =$ _____ °

$c =$ _____ °

$d =$ _____ °

/4

4. A small metal bar in the shape of a cuboid has both length and width equal to 2 cm and a depth of 4 cm.

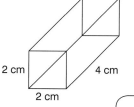

   a) Find the complete surface area of the metal bar.

       Surface area = _____ _____

   b) Find the volume of the metal bar. Volume = _____ _____

/4

5. Solve these equations.

   a) $2x - 9 = 45$ $x =$ _____

   b) $4x + 3 = 6x - 13$ $x =$ _____

   c) $5 - x = 8$ $x =$ _____

/3

6. A cube is cut in half to form two identical cuboids. Which of these statements can we say **for certain**? Answer true or false.

   a) The volume of each cuboid is half that of the original cube. _____

   b) The total surface area of each cuboid is half that of the original cube.

       _____

   c) There are only three ways the cube can be cut in this way. _____

/3

7. This pie-chart shows the proportion of the UK parliament after the 2010 general election.

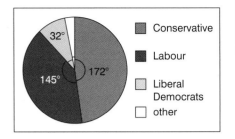

- **a)** What fraction of the new parliament consists of Liberal Democrat MPs?

  Give your answer as a simplified fraction.

  _____

- **b)** What is the percentage (to the nearest whole number) of Conservative MPs?

  _____

- **c)** What is the percentage of MPs that belong to none of the three main parties?

  _____

/3

8. Find the missing angles in the following diagram:

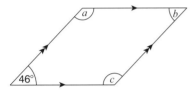

$a =$ _____ °

$b =$ _____ °

$c =$ _____ °

/3

9. **a)** A circle and a square have equal areas.

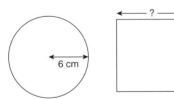

The radius of the circle is 6 cm, find the length (to 3 s.f.) of one side of the square.

_____ cm

- **b)** Another circle and square have the same perimeter. The radius of the circle is 6 cm.

  Find (to 3 s.f.) one side of the square. _____ cm

/2

10.

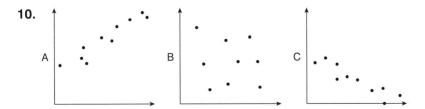

Which of these scatter diagrams (A, B or C) is most likely to show:

- **a)** how the value of a computer varies with its age?   Scatter diagram _____

- **b)** How an employer's salary varies with his or her shoe size?   Scatter diagram _____

c) How ice-cream sales vary with temperature? Scatter diagram _____

d) How the value of a house varies with its age? Scatter diagram _____

11. Hannah and Lily play a game that involves rolling dice. Lily's dice is a **fair** dice. /4

a) Complete the probability table below (using fractions) by finding the probability Lily has of rolling each number:

Number	1	2	3	4	5	6
Probability	$\frac{1}{6}$					

b) Hannah cheats by rolling a **biased** dice. The probability of her rolling anything from 2 to 5 is the same as Lily's. However, she is twice as likely to roll a 6 as a 1. Complete the probability table below (again using fractions) showing the probability Hannah has of rolling each number:

Number	1	2	3	4	5	6
Probability						

12. *Simplycarz* rents out small cars, charging a fixed price plus an additional charge per day.

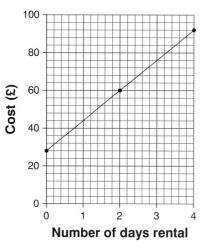

From the cost graph, state:

a) the fixed price £ _____

b) the additional price charged per day

£ _____

/2

13. In the following diagram, the radius of each circle is 5 cm.

a) Find (to 3 s.f.) the area of one of the circles.

_____ cm²

/3

b) Calculate the shaded area.

_____ cm²

/40

PAPER 7

1. Complete the calculations and reasons given below.
   The straight lines RABS and TCU are parallel.

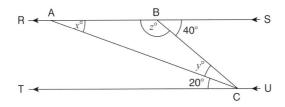

   a) $x =$ _____ °

   because _____

   b) $y + 20 = 40$

   because _____

   so $y =$ _____ °

   c) What is the mathematical name given to triangles like ABC? _____

   /3

2. A PC projector shows an image of a right-angled triangle on the screen.
   The ratio of its base to its height is 2 : 3.

   a) When the base of the image is 24 cm, what is its height? _____ cm

   b) The PC projector is moved; the height is now 30 cm.

   What is the area of this image of the right-angled triangle? _____ _____

   /3

3. Tony does a newspaper round for $1\frac{3}{4}$ hours each day.

   He does this for 5 days a week. How many hours a week is this? _____ hours

   /1

4. Use the fact that $a \propto b$ to help you complete this table of values.

a	5	6		35
b	12.5		67.5	87.5

   /2

5. This is a quadrilateral. It has diagonals AC and BD.

   In which quadrilaterals are the diagonals:

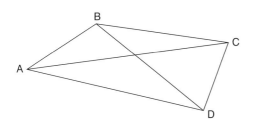

   a) always inside?

   _____

   b) Always the same length?

   _____

   c) Always cut each other at right angles?

   _____

   /3

6. When $x = 2m$ and $x = 3n$:

    a) Write down, in terms of x, the value of:

        (i) $4m + 3n$ _____   (ii) $12n$ _____

    b) Which of these statements are false (✗) and which are true (✓)?

        $n > m$ _____ $9n = 6m$ _____

        $3n - 2m = 0$ _____ $2x = 2m + 3n$ _____   /4

7. Put these patterns into groups each having the same ratio of Xs to Os.
You will not need to use all the groupings on the lines.

    A: XXOOO   B: OXXXO   C: OXOXO   D: OXO

    E: XOO   F: OOXXOO   G: XOXOX   H: OOXXXOOXXX

    _____   _____   _____   _____   /2

8. Solve these equations.

    a) $\frac{x}{5} = 6$ $x =$ _____   **b)** $3x + 9 = 12$ $x =$ _____

    c) $24 \div x = 8$ $x =$ _____   /3

9. Write these fractions in order of size, smallest first.

         $\frac{1}{4}$ $\frac{19}{24}$ $\frac{4}{24}$ $\frac{7}{12}$ $\frac{9}{12}$ $\frac{15}{48}$ /1

    _____

10. Andrea and Tim are on holiday in a big city. Andrea says that prices, for example for a
small bottle of water, are more expensive in shops closest to the centre. They gather
some information.
It is shown in this table.

Approximate distance from city centre (km)	0.0	0.1	0.2	0.3	0.4	0.5	0.6	0.7	0.8	0.9
Price of a bottle of water (£)	1.90	1.80	1.20	2.00	1.00	1.00	1.20	0.80	0.60	1.00

a) Plot their findings on this grid to make a scatter graph.

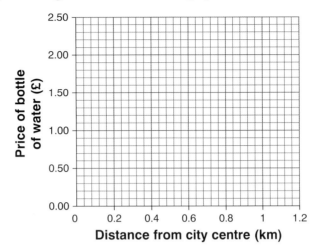

b) Is Andrea right?
Use the scatter graph to help you justify your answer.

_____

_____

_____

_____

/3

11. I think of a number, square it and add the original number. The answer is 90.

What number was I first thinking of? _____

/1

12. Find the missing numbers.

a) $\frac{1}{3} + \frac{1}{4} + \frac{1}{5} =$ _____

b) _____ $\times 7 = 5\frac{3}{5}$

c) _____ $\div 8 = \frac{3}{4}$

d) (_____)$^2 = \frac{9}{25}$

/4

13. Estimate the area and perimeter of this teardrop
by taking π to take the approximate value of 3.

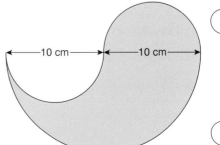

a) Perimeter = _____ cm

b) Area = _____ cm^2

/2

14.

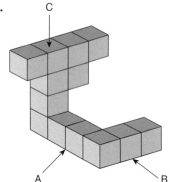

This model is made from centimetre cubes.

On a separate sheet of squared paper, draw and label the three views looking along directions A, B and C.

/3

15. Three cards labelled X, Y and Z are arranged in a line.

a) How many different arrangements are possible?

_____

b) How many different arrangements are possible with 4 differently lettered cards?

_____

/2

16. Here are three rows showing the formulae used in a spreadsheet:

◇	A	B	C	D	E	F	G	H	I
1	3	1	=A1+B1	=B1+C1	=C1+D1	=D1+E1	=E1+F1	=F1+G1	=G1+H1
2	3	=2*A2	=2*B2	=2*C2	=2*D2	=2*E2	=2*F2	=2*G2	=2*H2
3	3	=A3-2	=B3-2	=C3-2	=D3-2	=E3-2	=F3-2	=G3-2	=H3-2

Fill in the blank cells with the correct numbers.

◇	A	B	C	D	E	F	G	H	I
1	3	1							
2	3								
3	3								

/3

/40

PAPER 8

1. Complete these calculations.

   a) $\dfrac{5}{8} + \dfrac{2}{3} = $ _____

   b) $1\dfrac{3}{5} - \dfrac{3}{4} = $ _____

   /2

2. Write these numbers in ascending order.

   0.629   0.069   0.631   0.692   0.609   0.6   0.61

   /1

   _____

3. Sarah sells doughnuts at d pence each and apples at a pence each. Jo buys 2 doughnuts and 4 apples.

   a)   Write a formula for the total cost (C). _____

   b)   She pays with a £5 note. Write an expression for the amount of change she will get.

   /2

   _____

4. Find the missing angles in these shapes.

   $a = $ _____

   $b = $ _____

   $c = $ _____

   $d = $ _____

   $e = $ _____

   $f = $ _____

   $g = $ _____

   $h = $ _____

   /4

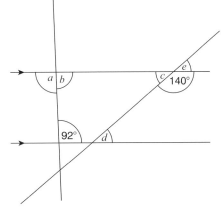

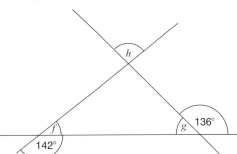

5. Complete these calculations.

    a) $6 + 3 \times 2 =$ _____

    b) $(3 + 6)^2 - 6 =$ _____

    c) $20 - 2^2 \times 3 + 8 \div 2 =$ _____

/3

6. Farmer Fred has 20 cows, 50 sheep, 45 chickens and 15 ducks.

    a)   What is the ratio of cows : sheep : ducks : chickens in its simplest form?

    _____

    b)   What is the ratio of birds : other animals in its simplest form?

    _____

/4

7. On a separate sheet of paper, use a pair of compasses to construct a triangle with sides 8 cm, 10 cm and 6 cm. Use your protractor to measure the angles in the triangle. Write the angles on the answer line.

_____

/1

8. $56 \times 79 = 4424$

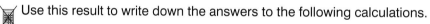 Use this result to write down the answers to the following calculations.

    a) $4424 \div 79 =$ _____

    b) $5.6 \times 7.9 =$ _____

    c) $0.56 \times 790 =$ _____

/3

9. Ivan needs to collect data on where his classmates went on holiday during the summer. On a separate sheet of paper, design a suitable data collection sheet he could use.

/2

10. a)   Kerry thinks of a number n. She divides it by 4 and then takes away 2. Her answer is 5.

      Write an equation and solve it to find Kerry's number.

    _____

    b)   Three bananas cost 90p more than just one. Write an equation and solve

      it to find the cost of one banana. _____

/3

11. The table shows the ages of people watching an animated film at the cinema.

Display this data in a labelled pie chart.

age	frequency
under 10	90
11 – 20	20
21 – 30	5
31 – 50	35
over 50	30

/2

12. Eight kilometres is approximately equal to five miles. Complete the following:

24 km = _____ miles

4 km = _____ miles

30 miles = _____ km

200 miles = _____ km

/2

13. a) Calculate the area of the face ABC.

_____

b) Calculate the volume of the prism.

_____

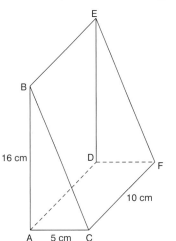

/2

14. Beryl and Eric are playing a game. Beryl tosses a coin and Eric rolls a dice. Beryl wins if she gets a head and Eric gets a 5 or a 6. Eric wins if Beryl gets a tail and he gets an even number.

coin\ dice	1	2	3	4	5	6
H	H1					
T					T5	

Complete the table and use it to work out:

a) the probability of Beryl winning _____

b) the probability of Eric winning. _____

c) Is the game fair? _____

/3

15. Write the names of these shapes in the correct place on the two-way table. The first one has been done for you.

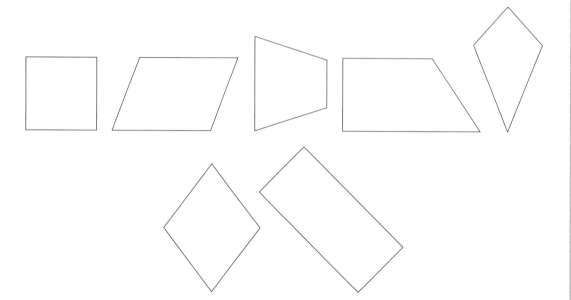

	2 pairs of parallel sides	1 or 0 pairs of parallel sides
equal length diagonals	square,	
unequal diagonals		

/3

16. Calculate the mean of these weights. Give your answer to 2 d.p.

3.2 kg   4.2 kg   2.8 kg   2.9 kg   3.7 kg   2.8 kg   3.7 kg

_____

/1

17. Solve these equations.

a) $2x - 7 = 3$ _____

b) $\frac{x}{2} + 4 = 9$ _____

/2

/40

PAPER 9

1. Write these fractions in ascending order.

$$\frac{1}{2} \qquad \frac{19}{20} \qquad \frac{3}{4} \qquad \frac{9}{10} \qquad \frac{7}{8}$$

2. **a)** Jon buys a new bike for £180. A year later he sells it for £72. Work out his actual loss and his percentage loss. _____

   b) Jon's father buys an old table for £150 and then sells it in an auction for £210. What is his percentage profit? _____

3. Here is the time (in minutes) that seven of Iain's friends spent on their last maths homework.

   | 37 | 32 | 24 | 5 | 42 | 25 | 39 |

   Calculate the mean and the median for this data.

   a) mean _____ **b)** median _____

   c) Which average do you think is the best one to use? _____

4. Draw all the lines of symmetry on each of these shapes.

    8

5. Ian and Fahra are cleaning cars. Ian works for 3 hours and Fahra for 2 hours 30 minutes. Altogether they earn £33 pounds which they divide in the ratio of hours worked.

   a) Write the ratio of time worked by Ian to time worked by Fahra in its simplest form.

   _____

   b) How much money did Fahra take home? _____

6. Write a pair of brackets in the following calculations (if needed) in order to make them correct.

   a) $2 \times 3^2 + 5 \times 4 = 112$

   b) $2 \times 3^2 + 5 \times 4 = 38$

   c) $2 \times 3^2 + 5 \times 4 = 56$

7. The formula to convert temperature measured on the Celsius scale, °C, to the Fahrenheit scale, °F, is:

$$F = \frac{9C}{5} + 32$$

a) A temperature of 57.8 °C was recorded in Libya in 1922. What was this in Fahrenheit to the nearest degree? _____

b) A temperature of −89 °F was recorded in Antarctica in 1983. Convert this to °C to the nearest degree. _____

/2

8. Jack is painting a round table top. The table has a diameter of 1.2 m. Calculate the area of the table in m² and cm². _____

/2

9. Sumera has designed this question for her project about leisure activities. "Exercise is good for you. Do you agree?"

a) What is wrong with her question? Design a better question to use.

_____

b) Sumera decides to take her new question and ask people outside the sports centre on a Wednesday morning. Why could this give biased results?

_____

/2

10. On this isometric grid, draw a cuboid with length 4 cm, width 3 cm and height 2 cm.

/1

11. a) Estimate the answer to this calculation. $\dfrac{(31.4 + 4.9)}{4.8}$ _____

b) Use your calculator to work out the correct answer. _____

c) Round your answer to 1 d.p. _____

/3

12. Rotate this shape 90° clockwise with centre of rotation (0,0)

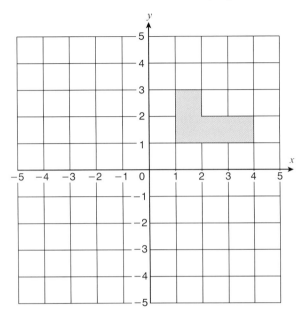

/1

13. For each of these sequences, write down the 10th term and an expression for the nth term.

a) 5   7   9   11 _____

b) 22   25   28   31 _____

/4

14. Complete the following table.

	number of pairs of equal sides	number of axes of symmetry	order of rotational symmetry
square	all 4 equal		
rectangle	2 pairs		
parallelogram			
trapezium			
isosceles trapezium			
kite			
rhombus			
arrowhead (delta)			

/3

15. Complete the following measurements.

2.4 m = _____ cm = _____ mm

3.8 km = _____ m = _____ cm

79 mm = _____ cm

5.3 kg = _____ g

3 cm² = _____ mm²

/2

16. Match each scatter graph to the correct pair of variables.

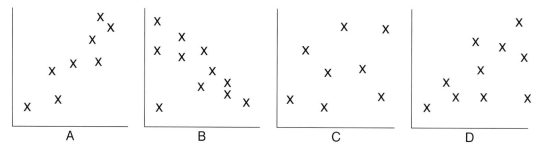

| A | B | C | D |

a) Maths test result and length of hair. _____

b) Height and weight of elephants. _____

c) Level of pollution in a river and number of healthy fish. _____

/2

17. Here is a graph of $y = x^2$.
Use the graph to find:

a) the value of y when $x = 2.5$

_____

b) the values of x when $y = 8$

_____

/2

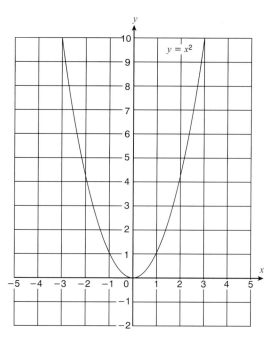

18. Complete this two-way table showing people using a country lane one Sunday afternoon.

	adults	children	total
on foot	15	8	
bike	4		10
horse	5	4	
pedal car		1	1
motor-bike		0	
total			54

a) What is the modal method of transport? _____

b) What is the probability that a person, chosen at random, is walking?

_____

/2

/40

PAPER 10

1. Write these numbers in order, smallest first.

$$\frac{7}{11} \qquad \frac{29}{61} \qquad \frac{9}{13} \qquad \frac{5}{9} \qquad 0.492$$

/1

2. Calculate the distance from the origin to the point (6, 7) on a square centimetre grid.

_____ cm

/1

3. a) The two shaded rectangles have equal areas.

Find x. _____ cm

b) What value will x take if the perimeters of the two shaded rectangles are the same?

_____ cm

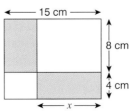

/2

4. A space-craft is travelling at 25000 mph.

   a) How far does it travel in a day? _____ miles

   b) The closest Mars gets to Earth is 36 million miles. How long would it take the
space-craft to travel this distance? _____

5. Fill in the blanks, using numbers in the box.

0.05	10	25	50

_____ × _____ = 1250   _____ ÷ _____ = 200   _____ × _____ = 1.25

_____ ÷ _____ = 0.005   _____ ÷ _____ = 1000

6. The price of petrol is rising very rapidly. One month it was £1.20 a litre. The next
month it went up by 10% and by a further 10% the following month.

What was the overall percentage increase for the two months? _____ %

7. The sum of four consecutive numbers, x, $x + 1$, $x + 2$ and $x + 3$ is less than 100.

   a) Write down and solve this inequality. _____ _____

   b) What are the largest possible four consecutive numbers that sum to less than 100?
_____

8. On a separate piece of squared paper draw a grid with values of x and y from -4 to 4.

   a) Draw the graphs of each of these equations.

      (i) $y = 2x + 1$ (ii) $x - y = 1$

   b) Use your graphs to solve the simultaneous equations $y = 2x + 1$ and $x - y = 1$

      $x =$ _____ $y =$ _____

9. A stopwatch is accurate to 0.1 seconds. It records the time for a race as 10.1 seconds.

The actual race time was therefore between _____ seconds and _____ seconds.

10. There are two fair 6-sided dice, one black and the other white.
The black one has faces marked 1, 2, 3, 3, 4 and 5.
The white one has faces marked 2, 3, 4, 4, 5 and 6.

   a) Use a table or diagram to help you list all the equally likely outcomes when the two
dice are thrown.

b) What is the probability of getting a double 3? _____

c) What is the most likely total when the two numbers on the dice are added?

_____ /3

11. This table shows the January rainfall, in mm, at Heathrow Airport for the last 64 years.

January Rainfall (r mm)	Frequency (number of years)
$0 < r \le 20$	11
$20 < r \le 40$	11
$40 < r \le 60$	13
$60 < r \le 80$	21
$80 < r \le 100$	4
$100 < r \le 120$	4

a) Calculate an estimate of the mean rainfall at Heathrow Airport in January.

_____ mm

b) Estimate the range of the rainfall figures.

_____ mm

c) Which is the modal class of these rainfall figures?

_____ mm /3

12. James drops a full litre carton of milk on the kitchen floor. It all goes over the floor making a puddle. The depth of the milk puddle is about 2 mm. What is the area of the milk puddle?

_____ /2

13.

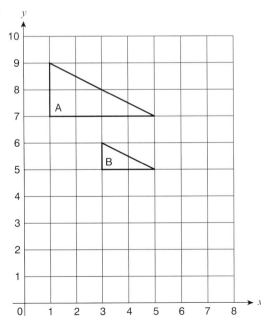

a) Describe completely the transformation that maps triangle A onto triangle B.

_____

b) What properties remain the same when A is mapped onto B?

_____

/3

Level 7

14. Here are some equations. Put them into groups of matching equations.

[1] $ax = by + c$ [2] $b = \dfrac{ax + c}{y}$ [3] $x = \dfrac{by + c}{a}$ [4] $c = ax + by$

[5] $ax = by - c$ [6] $y = \dfrac{ax - c}{b}$ [7] $y = \dfrac{ax + c}{b}$ [8] $ax = c - by$

[9] $b = \dfrac{c - ax}{y}$ [10] $c = ax - by$

/2

15.

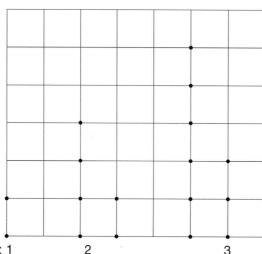

Shape: 1   2   3

The pattern of these shapes continues.

a) How many dots are in shape 4?

_____

b) How many dots are in the nth shape?

_____

c) Write down the first three terms of the sequence made from the difference in the number of spots between each shape.

_____ _____ _____

/3

16. On a separate piece of graph paper, draw the y-axis going from -3 to 10 and the x-axis from -5 to 5.

a) Draw the curve represented by $y = x^2 - 2x$.

b) On the same grid draw the straight line $y = x + 4$

c) Write down where the curve and straight line intersect. _____

/3

17. On a separate piece of paper make a full-size drawing of this triangle. Measure the angles A and B.

A = _____ °

B = _____ °

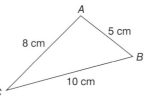

/2

/2

18. Expand the brackets and simplify these expressions.

a) $(x + 2)^2 =$ _____   **b)** $(x - 2)(x + 3) =$ _____

/40

PAPER 11

1. Use algebra to solve this puzzle.
   "The sum of a and twice b is 17 and b is one more than double a. Find a and b."

   $a =$ _____ $b =$ _____

2. A museum display room is rectangular measuring 12 m by 8 m.
   There is a motion sensor in the middle of the room. It has range of 5 m.
   On a separate piece of paper, draw the display room to a scale of 1 cm to 1 m.
   Shade the locus of all the points not covered by the motion sensor.

/1

3. This prism has an isosceles triangle as its cross-section.

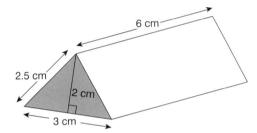

   a) Calculate the surface area of the prism.

   _____ cm²

   b) Calculate the volume of the prism.

   _____ cm³

/2

4. For the set of numbers 8, 5, 4, 3, and x, the values of the mean, mode and
   median are the same.
   What is the value of x? _____

/1

5. Find all the whole number solutions to $8 \le 2x < 16$ _____

/1

6. a) Calculate the area of the square ABCD.   _____ cm²

   b) Calculate the length BD.   _____ cm

/2

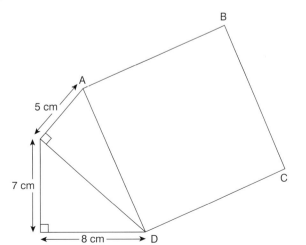

7. Multiply out and simplify each of these expressions.

a) $(x + 1)(x - 5) =$ _____

b) $(x + 2)^2 =$ _____

/2

8. Kurt is collecting information about the number of screens (TV plus computer) the members of his athletics club have at home. Here is his tally chart. He wants to work out a figure for the average number of screens members have.

Number of screens	Tally
0	
1	###
2	### //
3	### ### /
4	### ### ///
5	###
6	///
7	//

Kurt's friend Kathy says the average is 3.5 screens, but Kurt reckons it is 4 screens. In fact they are both correct.

Kathy is correct because the _____ is 3.5.

Kurt is also correct because

_____

/2

9. These are three bridges on a canal. The distance from Bridge 21 to Bridge 22 is given as 7 km and the distance from Bridge 22 to Bridge 23 is 12 km.

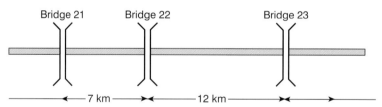

Bridge 21   Bridge 22   Bridge 23

7 km   12 km

a) The actual distance between Bridges 21 and 22 is between

_____ km and _____ km

b) The actual distance between Bridge 21 and Bridge 23 is between

_____ km and _____ km

/2

10. In tower-running people run up the stairs of tall buildings. Here are some female records.

Tower	Steps	Time
Empire State, USA	1576	11 min. 23s
Sears Building, USA	2109	15 min. 18s
Emirate Tower, Dubai	1334	10 min. 50s
Taipei 101, Taiwan	2046	14 min. 20s

a) How many steps a second did the female record holder run up the Empire State?

_____ steps per second

b) How many steps per second was the fastest rate for these female tower runners?

Which tower was it? _____ at _____ steps per second

/3

11. Complete these calculations.

a) ____ $+ 1\frac{1}{2} + \frac{1}{4} + \frac{3}{8} = 3\frac{1}{4}$

b) $\frac{5}{9} \div$ ____ $= \frac{2}{9}$

c) ____ $\times \frac{1}{4} = \frac{1}{6}$

/3

12. Some students are experimenting finding the median number shown when three fair 6-sided dice are thrown. Here are their results.

Median number	1	2	3	4	5	6
Frequency	3	10	11	13	9	4

a) According to the results above what is the least probable median number?

_____

b) What is the experimental probability of getting a median of 3? _____

c) What is the experimental probability of not getting a median of 6? _____

/3

13. Find the value of this expression $\frac{6.1^3 - 1.2^2}{3.9^3 - 0.9^2}$

Give your answer to 2 d.p. _____

/1

14. The winning rule in a dice game is $r + 3b$, where r is the number showing on the red dice and b the number showing on the blue dice.
Both dice are fair 4-sided dice and $r + 3b \leq 10$.
List all the possible winning throws.

_____

/1

15. By using square roots ($\sqrt{\ }$) make the statements below true.
For example, $4 + 4 = 4$ can be made true by $\sqrt{4} + \sqrt{4} = 4$

a) $1 + 9 = 16$ _____

b) $16 + 4 = 36$ _____

/2

16. A photocopier has a fault; it reduces the height of a copy by 5% and enlarges the width by 10%.
A rectangular image 10 cm high by 8 cm in width is copied on the machine.
By how much difference in area will the photocopy of the rectangle image be?

It will be _____ by _____ cm²

/2

17. Complete these calculations, $\approx$ means "approximately equal to".

a) $\dfrac{1.19 + 2.1^2}{3.94 - 3.83} \approx$ _____ $=$ _____

b) $(15.7 + 10.1) \div 4.86 \approx$ _____ $=$ _____

/2

18. Make a the subject of the formula, $w = \dfrac{a + b + c + d}{4}$ _____

/1

19. Which of these points are on, above or below the curve given by $y = x^2 + x - 1$?
(Hint: you will probably need to draw the curve.)

$(0, 0)$ $(0, -1)$ $(-1, 0)$ $(2, 4)$ $(1, 1)$ $(4, 5)$

On the curve _____

Above the curve _____

Below the curve _____

/2

20. Rick wants to buy an E240 notebook PC. He looks on the Internet for some prices.
He finds these, in £s.

95	122	108	86	103	82	77	75	112	118
102	104	116	85	122	87	100	104	97	107
69	78	125	109	99	105	99	101	85	87

a) On a separate piece of paper, put the prices into a grouped frequency table.
Use seven groups starting with £60.

b) Plot the prices on a clearly labelled frequency polygon.

/3

21. For cars travelling at normal speed, the air drag is proportional to the speed of the car squared.
Complete this table showing how drag, in newtons, changes with speed for a particular car.

Speed (km/h)	0	20	40	60	80
Drag (newtons)	0	8	32	72	

/1

22. Here are some triangles drawn on squared paper. Put them into groups of triangles which are similar.

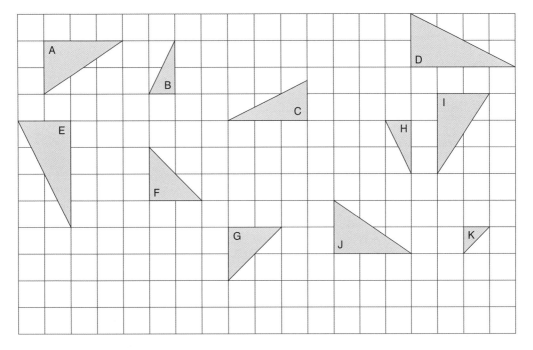

_____

_____

/1

/40

PAPER 12

1. The sides of a cuboid are whole numbers of centimetres. The areas of the three different-sized faces are 6 cm², 8 cm² and 12 cm². What is the size and volume of the cuboid?

   _____cm by _____cm by _____cm and volume _____

   /3

2. This is the scale on a garden thermometer.

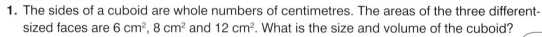

   a) Frank uses the thermometer to measure inside his greenhouse.
   He says it is 21 °C. Between which two values could the temperature lie?

   _____ °C and _____ °C

   b) Frank measures the outside temperature using the same thermometer.
   He says it is −5 °C. Between which two temperatures could the difference in temperature between the outside and inside the greenhouse lie?

   _____ °C and _____ °C

   /2

3. A gardener has four water sprinklers. Each one waters all the ground within a radius of 5 m.
   She has a square lawn measuring 8 m by 8 m and she puts a sprinkler at each corner.
   On a separate piece of paper, draw a scale diagram of the lawn, using a scale of 1 cm to represent 1 m.
   Shade in the area of lawn which gets no water.

   /2

4. This is a sketch of the side wall of a swimming pool.
   The swimming pool is 10 m wide.

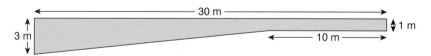

   a) What volume of water can the swimming pool hold? _____

   b) The pool is filled at 0.8 m³/minute. How long does it take to fill the pool? _____

   c) A litre of water has a mass of 1 kg.
   How many tonnes is the water in the swimming pool? (1 tonne is 1000 kg)

   _____ tonnes

   /5

5. Calculate $13 + 13^2 + 13^3 + 13^4 + 13^5$, give your answer to the nearest 100.

_____   /1

6. Calculate the perimeter of this rhombus.

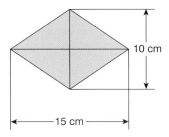

_____ cm

/1

7. Amy has a biased spinner. Here are the results of some trials.

Number	1	2	3	4	5
Frequency	26	19	5	16	32

a) Use the results to estimate the probability of getting a 3 with the spinner after one spin.

_____

b) What could Amy do to estimate more accurately the probability of getting a 3?

_____   /2

/1

8. Make a the subject of this formula: $y = ax + b$ _____

9. A laboratory is testing a greenfly spray for roses. Some rose plants are divided into two groups. One group was not treated, the other was sprayed. This table shows the results of the tests.

	Infected with greenfly	Not infected with greenfly	Total
Sprayed	318	209	527
Not sprayed	136	47	183
Total	454	256	710

a) What percentage of rose plants which were infected were sprayed? _____%

b) Does your answer to a) give a good impression about the effectiveness of the spray? Compare the effectiveness of the spray by comparing sprayed with not-sprayed roses.

The proportion of sprayed which were infected is _____%

and the proportion of not sprayed which were infected is _____%   /3

10. Put the correct symbol, $=$, $>$, or $<$ on the line that will fit the two previous statements, if this is not possible put a ✗ meaning "cannot be certain".

If $a < b$ and $c > b$ then a _____ c.

If $c < b$ and $a > c$ then b _____ a.

If $a > b$ and $c > a$ then b _____ c.

If $c > b$ and $b > a$ then a _____ c.

/2

11. Complete this working to find a rough answer to the original calculation.
 (Remember $\approx$ means "roughly equal to")

a) $\dfrac{15.176 \times 0.913}{102.8 \times 0.0311} \approx$ _____

b) $\dfrac{\sqrt{17} \times 3.1}{1.97 \times 2.1} \approx$ _____

/2

12. Write down the next two terms in each of these sequences.

a) $1\frac{7}{8}$ $2\frac{1}{4}$ $2\frac{5}{8}$ _____   _____

b) $8\frac{8}{9}$ $8\frac{1}{3}$ $7\frac{7}{9}$ _____   _____

/2

13. Find two consecutive whole numbers whose squares differ by 13. _____ _____

/1

14. In a process for silver-plating jewellery, the mass of silver deposited is proportional to the time for which the item of jewellery is plated. A 15 minute plating time deposits 1.2 g.

How much longer will it take to plate a total of 5 g of silver? _____ minutes

/1

15. Here are the maximum temperatures, °C, on May the 1ˢᵗ 2010 in the 20 largest US cities.

29	22	21	30	27	32	28	26	17	21
23	17	32	16	28	21	25	27	26	31

Temperature T(°C)	Tally	Frequency
$10 \le T < 15$		
$15 \le T < 20$		
$20 \le T < 25$		
$25 \le T < 30$		
$30 \le T < 35$		
$35 \le T < 40$		

a) Complete this grouped frequency table for these temperatures.

b) On a separate piece of paper, draw and label a frequency polygon showing the temperatures in the table.

c) Calculate the true mean of the temperatures and also the estimate of the mean calculated using the grouped frequency table.

(i) Mean temperature _____ °C

(ii) Estimated mean temperature _____ °C

/5

16. Some seeds were planted. A quarter of them did not germinate.

Of those that germinated $\frac{3}{4}$ failed to flower. What fraction of the original seeds flowered?

_____

/1

17. a) Complete this table of values for $y = x(x - 4)(x - 5)$.

x	0	1	2	3	4	5	6
$y = x(x - 4)(x - 5)$	0					0	12

b) On a separate piece of paper, draw the graph of $y = x(x - 4)(x - 5)$.

c) Use your graph to solve the equation $x(x - 4)(x - 5) = 12$. _____

/6

/40

PAPER 13

1. Pick any prime number greater than 3. Square your number, add 12, then find the remainder when you divide the answer by 12. Start with some other prime numbers. What do you notice?

_____

/1

2. A rectangular games pitch is measured to the nearest metre and found to be 93 m by 57 m. Given these measurements, between which two figures will the area of the field lie?

_____ m² and _____ m²

/1

3. Write down and solve each of these inequalities. Use x to represent the number.

a) Ten is less than twice the number.

_____ which has the solution _____

b) Seven added to the number gives a positive number.

_____ which has the solution _____

/2

55

4. A circle has a radius of 6 cm.

   a) On a separate piece of paper, sketch and label the locus of point P which moves so that it is always 1 cm away from the circumference of the circle.

   b) What is the area of the region in which P can move? (Take π = 3.1).

   _____

/3

5. On average a coat of gloss paint is about 0.1 cm thick. According to most decorating books a 5 litre tin of gloss paint covers about 20 m². Is this reasonable? Give some numbers and calculations to support your answer.

   _____ because _____

/1

6. Here are the lengths, in cm, of nine sticks.

   5   7   8   12   13   15   17   24   25

   Three right-angled triangles can be made using the sticks. Which ones form each triangle?

   a) _____   **b)** _____   **c)** _____

/2

7. An airline charges £210 for a flight to New York. From June 1st it will increase this fare by 13%, but it is offering a 4.5% discount on night flights.
How much will a night flight to New York cost on June 2nd? £ _____

/1

8. There are three whole numbers, a, b and c. Taken two at a time they add up to 8, 12 and 14.

   What are the three numbers? _____   _____   _____

/2

9. The formula for the volume, V cm³, of a sphere of radius r cm is given by the formula $V = \frac{4}{3}\pi r^3$.

   Estimate the volume of a sphere of radius 1.9 cm. _____ cm³

/1

10. The formula for finding the volume, V m³, of a triangular prism is $V = \frac{abc}{2}$, where a, b and c are in metres.

   a) Make a the subject of the above formula.

   _____

   b) This is a sketch of a float in the shape of a triangular prism. Each cubic metre of float will support and keep floating a load of 0.8 tonnes.

   What value should the length x be to support a load of 50 tonnes? _____ m

/2

11. Safiq experiments dropping a paper cup.
It may land right-way up, on its side or upside-down.
Here are his results.

Landing	Tally
Right-way up	///
On its side	### ### ### ### ### ### ### ///
Upside-down	### ### /

a) What is the probability that the next time the cup is dropped, it lands on its side? _____

b) If Safiq dropped the cup 100 times, about how many times would he expect it to land the right-way up?

_____

/2

12. Complete this multiplication grid.

×	$\frac{3}{4}$	$\frac{4}{7}$	$\frac{8}{9}$	
$1\frac{1}{2}$		$\frac{6}{7}$	$1\frac{1}{3}$	$\frac{3}{4}$
	$\frac{9}{16}$	$\frac{3}{7}$	$\frac{2}{3}$	$\frac{3}{8}$
$\frac{7}{8}$		$\frac{1}{2}$	$\frac{7}{9}$	$\frac{7}{16}$

/4

13. Write down all the whole numbers which fit **all** of these inequalities.

$-1 \leq x$ $\qquad$ $x < 2$ $\qquad$ $3x < 9$ $\qquad$ $2x > -4$ $\qquad$ _____

/1

14. Which of these points lay on the curve given by: $y = x^3 - 5x^2 + 5x$?

$(-2, 40)$ $\qquad$ $(-1, 11)$ $\qquad$ $(0, 0)$ $\qquad$ $(2, -4)$ $\qquad$ $(4, 4)$ $\qquad$ $(5, 25)$

_____

/1

15. Use your calculator to find the value correct to 1 decimal place of:

$$\frac{(1.3 - 0.9^2) \times (1.8^2 + 1.3^2)}{(0.12^3)}$$ _____

/1

16. A circular pond has a radius of 10 m.

a) What length of rope, to the nearest metre, will just go round the pond at a distance of 10 cm from its

edge? _____ m

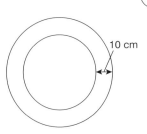

10 cm

b) What is the area of ground, to the nearest square metre, between the rope and the edge of the pond? _____ m²

 /2

17. Estimate these:

a) $\dfrac{\sqrt{17.01}}{\sqrt{3.9} \times \sqrt{4.1}} \approx$ _____

b) $\dfrac{1.95^3}{\sqrt{62.5}} \approx$ _____

c) $2\sqrt{80} + 1.97^2 \approx$ _____

 /3

18. Put these expressions into identical groups.

$(x + 2)(x - 6) + 12$ $\qquad$ $(x + 2)(x + 2)$ $\qquad$ $x^2 + 4$ $\qquad$ $(x - 1)(x + 1) + 5$

$x(x - 4)$ $\qquad$ $x^2 + 4x + 4$ $\qquad$ $x^2 - 4x$ $\qquad$ $x(x + 4) + 4(1 - x)$

_____

_____

/2

19. Find the coordinates of the point of intersection of the lines whose equations are

$2x - 3y = 11$ and $5x + 2y = 18$ $\quad$ (_____ , _____)

 /2

20. A number sequence is generated from these patterns of dots.

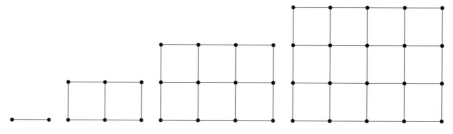

The first term is 2, the second term is 6, the third term is 12 and so on.

a) Write down the value of the 5th and 6th terms. _____ _____

b) Use the patterns in the dots to write down an expression for the nth term $T(n)$.

$T(n) =$ _____

/2

21. Match each of these curves with its equation.
   Choose from this list   [1] $y = x^2$ [2] $y = x^2 - 4$ [3] $y = x^2 + 4$ [4] $y = 4x^2$
   [5] $y = x^2 + 2$ [6] $y = x^2 + x + 1$ [7] $y = x^2 + x - 1$

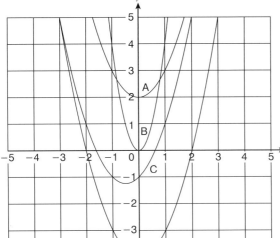

[A] _____

[B] _____

[C] _____

[D] _____

/2

22. Amy says

> The perimeter of a square multiplied by itself is proportional to the area of the same square.

Show whether or not Amy is right.
Write a word equation linking the (perimeter)² of a square and its area.

_____

_____

_____

/2

/40

PAPER 14

1. a) Nicholas and Alexandra decide to fly to Cyprus. The cost of a Simplejet flight from Manchester to Larnaca costs £80 before VAT is added at 17.5%. Finally, as they are booking online, the total cost is reduced by 5%. How much will the airline charge them overall?

£ _____

b) A return rail ticket from Inverness to Thurso costs £21.
Supposing the cost of rail travel rises by 5% each year, how much will the same ticket cost in three years time?

£ _____

/4

2. Find the areas of these shapes.

a) a parallelogram

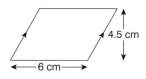

b) a trapezium

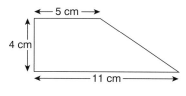

Area = _____ cm²

Area = _____ cm²

/2

3. 50 Year 10 pupils were asked how much time (to the nearest hour) they spent on their GCSE homework the previous evening. The results were as follows:

Time (hours)	0	1	2	3	4
No. of pupils	7	20	16	5	2

a) Draw a frequency polygon for this data on the axes below:

b) State the median time spent doing homework.

Median time = _____ hours

/4

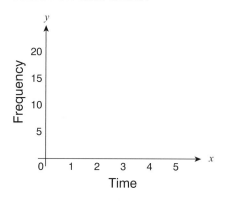

4. In the diagram, ABCD is a square.
Given AC = $\sqrt{32}$ cm, calculate:

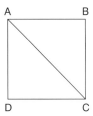

a) the length of AB _____ cm

b) the perimeter of the square _____ cm

c) the area of the square _____ cm

 /4

5. A string is fixed to two points, A and B, on a horizontal surface a fixed distance apart. The pencil is moved in such a way that the string is always kept taut.

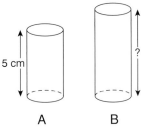

Could the pencil line possibly produce any of the following shapes?
Answer yes or no.

a) a straight line _____

b) a circle _____

c) an ellipse _____

d) a triangle _____

 /4

6. Solve these simultaneous equations.

a) $x + y = 19$ $x =$ _____

   $x - y = 13$ $y =$ _____

b) $2x - 3y = 7$ $x =$ _____

   $8x + y = 2$ $y =$ _____

/4

7.

A and B are similar cylinders (one is an enlargement of the other) and cylinder B holds twice as much water as cylinder A.

Calculate (to 3 s.f.) the height of the second cylinder.

 /2

_____ cm

8. a and b are two numbers bigger than 0. Consider the following statements and decide if they are ALWAYS true, SOMETIMES true, or NEVER true:

a) $a + b$ is greater than a _____

b) ab is greater than a _____

c) $a^2 b = b$ _____

d) a^2 is less than 0 _____

e) $\dfrac{a}{b} = \dfrac{b}{a}$ _____

/5

9. The volume of a sphere is given by Volume $= \dfrac{4}{3}\pi r^3$.

The radius of a tennis ball is measured as 3.2 cm to the nearest mm.

a) Find (to 3 s.f.) the minimum and maximum possible values of the volume of a tennis ball.

Minimum volume = _____ cm³

Maximum volume = _____ cm³

b) The volume of a basketball is measured to be 200 cm³ to the nearest cubic centimetre. Find (to 3 s.f.) the minimum and maximum possible values of its radius.

Minimum radius = _____ cm

Maximum radius = _____ cm

/4

10. By rounding each given number to one significant figure, estimate values for the following:

a) $\dfrac{6.32 \times 5.88}{0.47}$ _____

b) $\sqrt{\dfrac{475}{0.21}}$ _____

c) $0.12 \times 0.21 \times 415$ _____

/3

11. In the diagram below, length BD = 6 cm and length AE = 10 cm.
Triangle CBD is an enlargement of triangle CAE.

a) What is the scale factor of the enlargement, expressed as a simplified fraction? _____

b) If CE = 25 cm, calculate the length of CD

_____ cm

c) If AB = 3 cm, calculate the length of BC.

_____ cm

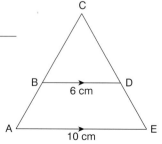

/4

/40

PAPER 15

1. A ladder of length 6 m is placed 1.9 m from the base of a wall.

   a) How far (to 3 s.f.) up the wall does the ladder reach? _____ m

   b) The same ladder is now moved so that it reaches a height of 5.3 m.
       How far (to 3 s.f.) is the ladder now from the base of the wall?

       _____ m

   /2

2. A biased dice is rolled 120 times and the top number shown recorded.
   The results are shown below.

No. on dice	1	2	3	4	5	6
Frequency	20	30	17	21	22	10

   a) How many times would you expect each number to appear if the dice was a fair one?

       _____

   b) The dice is rolled one more time. Calculate the probability of rolling a 6.

       _____

   /2

3. A survey was taken to see how long 25 Year 9 pupils spend on the internet each evening.
   The results are shown in the following grouped frequency table:

Time x minutes	Frequency	Class mid-interval	Frequency x mid-interval
$0 \leq x < 10$	4		
$10 \leq x < 30$	7		
$30 \leq x < 60$	8		
$60 \leq x < 120$	6		

   a) Complete the final two columns.

   b) Calculate an estimate for the mean length of time spent on the internet.

       _____ min

   c) State the modal class _____

   d) State the range of times _____ min

   /5

4. The speed of light is 300000000 m/s.

a) How far (in km) can light travel in one-fiftieth of a second? _____ km

b) How far (in km) can light travel in one-millionth of a second? _____ km

c) The average distance from the earth to the sun is 150000000 km. How long does it take for light to travel from the sun to the earth? _____ min _____ sec   /4

5. Patrick and Marwan play a game of darts. After several games, their respective mean scores and ranges are calculated. The results are as follows:

Player	Mean	Range
Patrick	30	15
Marwan	20	5

State whether the following statements are true or false.

a) Patrick is the most consistent darts player.   _____

b) Patrick, on average, obtains the highest scores.   _____

c) Marwan must have scored the lowest single throw from the two players.

_____

d) Marwan could not have scored more than 25 with a single throw.

_____   /4

6. a) The line $2x - 5y = 30$ crosses the x-axis at A and the y-axis at B.
Find the coordinates of both A and B.

A (_____, _____)   B (_____, _____)

b) Find the coordinate C where the same line intersects another line given by the equation $y = x$

C (_____, _____)   /3

7. a) The area of a triangle can be shown to be $\sqrt{s(s-a)(s-b)(s-c)}$, where a, b and c are the lengths of the three sides of the triangle and s is half the perimeter of the triangle. Calculate the area of the triangle (to 3 s.f.) when $a = 5$ cm, $b = 8$ cm and $c = 10$ cm.

Area = _____ cm²

b) Given $\frac{1}{p} + \frac{1}{q} = \frac{1}{r}$, find r when $p = 3$ and $q = 6$. $r =$ _____

8. a) Calculate the volume of the chocolate bar container shown. _____ cm³

b) A special festive edition of the bar is produced, with its length, height and depth all doubled in size. How much more chocolate than the original will it hold?

_____ times as much.

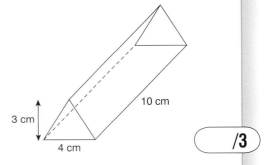

9. Write the limits of accuracy of the following measurements. The first one has been done for you.

a) 12 cm to the nearest cm.   Limits are 11.5 cm $\leq$ 12 cm $<$ 12.5 cm

b) 30 kg to the nearest kg.   Limits are _____ $\leq$ 30 kg $<$ _____

c) 24600 tonnes to the nearest tonne.   Limits are _____ $\leq$ 24600 tonnes $<$ _____

d) 100 m to the nearest 10 m.   Limits are _____ $\leq$ 100 m $<$ _____

e) 100 m to the nearest 5 m.   Limits are _____ $\leq$ 100 m $<$ _____

10. A coin rolls along a flat horizontal surface.
Sketch a diagram showing the locus of the set of points P if:

a) P is initially situated at the centre of the coin.

_____

b) P is initially at the top of the coin.

/4

11. **a)** The nth term of a sequence is given by the formula $3n^2 + 1$.

Write down the first five terms in the sequence. _____

b) i) Consider the sequence given by 5, 8, 13, 20, 29, ...

Find a formula for the nth term in this sequence. _____

ii) Write down the 50th term in this sequence. _____

/4

12. Marina deposits £100 in an overseas savings account, earning an interest rate of 10%.

After how many complete years will she have doubled her money? _____

/2

/40

PAPER 16

1. Write the following numbers in ascending order.

| 0.64 | $\frac{2}{3}$ | 69% | 0.609 | $\frac{3}{5}$ | 73% |

_____

2. Sumera is doing a 'bug' count for her science project. In one soil sample she counts the following: 10 ants, 4 spiders, 3 beetles and 1 worm. If she picks a creature at random, what is the probability of her choosing:

a) A beetle? _____

b) A spider? _____

/3

c) A creature with legs? _____

3. Find the missing angles.
Show your working and explain your reasoning clearly.

$x =$ _____°

because _____

$y =$ _____°

because _____

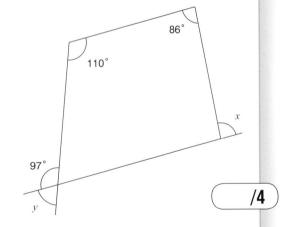

/4

4. Marie has music, videos and photographs stored on her mp3 player.
She has 32 GB of music files, 24 GB of video files, 8 GB of photos and 16 GB of empty space.

a) Write the ratio of music : video : photos in its simplest form.

_____

b) What fraction of the whole memory is empty space. Write your answer in its simplest form.

_____

/5

c) What percentage of the memory is photos? _____

5. Here are two similar triangles.
Calculate the lengths TU and PR.

TU = _____

PR = _____

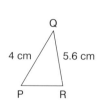

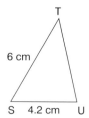

6. a) Calculate $22 - 3^2 \times 2$

_____

b) Work out the value of $ac - b^2$ when:

i) $a = 6$, $b = 4$ and $c = 7$ _____

ii) $a = -2$, $b = 3$ and $c = -4$ _____

/3

7. The table shows the wages earned and hours worked by ten students from Year 12 who have Saturday jobs.

hours worked	2	1.5	3	6	5	4.5	2.5	6	3.5	3
wages (£)	12	9	17	33	39	31	15	39	25	30

a) Use a separate sheet of graph paper to plot this information on a scatter graph.

b) Describe the relationship between hours worked and wages.

_____

c) Draw a line of best fit on your graph and use it to estimate the wages of a student

who works for 5 hours. _____

/4

8. Sam and Jon are riding their bikes. Sam travels 4.5 km in exactly 20 minutes, Jon's bike has a speedometer which says he is travelling at 13 km/h. Who is riding faster and by how much? You must show your working.

/2

_____ by _____ km/h

9. Here is a triangular prism.

a) Find the area of triangle ABC.

_____

b) (i) Show how to calculate the length BC.

_____

(ii) Calculate the length BC.

_____

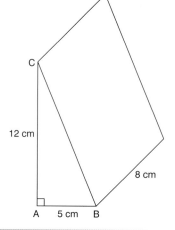

c) Calculate the surface area of the whole

prism. _____

/5

10. Liz hires a snowboard and helmet at her local snowdome.

> **Hire Charge**
> **Snowboard £5**
> **Helmet £1.50 per hour**

a) Write a formula to calculate the cost, C (£), of hiring equipment for h hours.

_____

b) Use your formula to work out how much Liz will pay if she stays for 3 hours.

£ _____

/2

11. a) Complete this grid for the equation $y = 2x + 4$

x	−2	−1	0	1	2
y					

b) On a separate piece of graph paper draw the line $y = 2x + 4$

/4

12. Use your calculator to work out:

$$14.7 \div (3.7 + 4.4)$$

Write down all the figures on the display and then round your answer to 1 decimal place.

_____ = _____

/2

13. Here is a number sequence.

$$15 \qquad 18 \qquad 21 \qquad 24$$

a) Write the next three numbers in the sequence.

_____

b) Write an expression for the nth term of this sequence.

_____

/3

/40

PAPER 17

1. Wilf watched two hours of television. During this time there were 5 commercial breaks each of 3 minutes.

   a) What is the ratio of programme time : commercials?

   _____

   b) If his neighbour watches the same channel for 4 hours every day for a week how many hours of commercials will he watch in a week?

   _____

   /2

2. Reflect shape A in the x-axis. Label the new shape B.
   Reflect shape B in the y-axis and label it C.
   What SINGLE transformation moves A directly on to C?

   _____

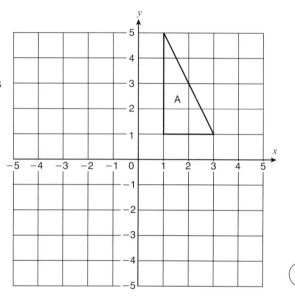

   /2

3. Sophie is making a tablecloth for a round table with a diameter of 2.3 m. The tablecloth will overlap the table by 25 cm all round.

   a) What will the diameter of the tablecloth be? _____

   b) The material for the cloth is cut off a roll that is 3 m wide and costs £15 per metre.
   How much will the material cost? _____

   c) Sophie will edge the tablecloth all round with ribbon which costs £4.50 per metre.
   How much ribbon will she need, and how much will she have to pay for the ribbon?

   _____

   /3

4. a) Round each number to 1 significant figure and estimate the value of

$\dfrac{54.6 \times 27.5}{0.49}$ _____

    b) Use a calculator to work out the correct answer, rounded to 1 decimal place.

_____ /3

5. A company who manufactures furniture increases all its prices because of increasing costs.

    a) A sofa increases from £380 to £437. What is the percentage increase?

_____

    b) A table originally costing £245 increases by 18%. What is its new price?

_____ /2

6. Sonja runs 100 m at her school sports day. The stopwatch gives her time as 15.4 s correct to the nearest tenth of a second. What are the fastest and slowest possible times she

could have actually run? _____ /2

7. a) How many lines of symmetry does this shape have?

_____

    b) On a separate sheet of paper show how the shape tessellates. Draw at least 6 more shapes.  /2

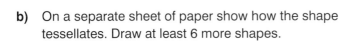

8. Work out the value of $2a^2 - 4\dfrac{b}{c}$ when:

    a) $a = 2$ $b = 6$ $c = 3$ _____

    b) $a = 8$ $b = 3$ $c = 6$ _____

    c) $a = -4$ $b = -10$ $c = 2.5$ _____ /2

9. On a separate sheet of paper draw a line 10 cm long. Accurately construct the locus of all the points 3 cm from this line. /2

10. Raoul and Susan are playing a game with home-made spinners and they test each spinner by throwing it 50 times. Here are their results.

Score	1	2	3	4	5	6
Raoul's	5	6	3	5	8	23
relative frequency	$\frac{5}{50} = 0.10$	$\frac{6}{50} = 0.12$				
Susan	0	16	5	10	0	19
relative frequency						

a) Calculate the relative frequencies of each score and complete the table.

b) What can you say about Susan's spinner? _____

c) If they have to get a 6 to start a game, who is most likely to begin? Can you be absolutely sure?

_____

/4

11. Solve these equations.

a) $2a + 5 = 29$ _____

b) $b^2 - 7 = 9$ _____

c) $c + 10 = 4c + 1$ _____

/3

12. Here is a sequence of numbers:

83 87 91 95

a) Write down the next three numbers in the sequence.

_____

b) Write down an expression for the nth term of this sequence.

_____

c) Write down the first 4 numbers in the sequence with n^{th} term $n^2 + 1$

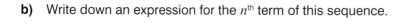

_____

/3

13. Ami is picking apples. Her ladder is 3.5 m long and the branch on the tree is 2.5 m high. How far from the bottom of the tree must she put the foot of her ladder? Give your answer to 2 significant figures.

/2

14. a) Tom is designing a questionnaire about homework. Design a question he could use to find how long his classmates spend on their maths homework.

b) Here are the responses to Tom's question "How many hours of homework do you get per week?"
Use a separate sheet of graph paper to show this data on a frequency diagram. Which is the modal class? What is the range of the data?

/6

number of hours	frequency
$0 \leq h < 2$	1
$2 \leq h < 4$	4
$4 \leq h < 6$	15
$6 \leq h < 8$	28
$8 \leq h < 10$	12

15. Will, Charlotte and Abigail were on a school trip. Will had three more sweets than Charlotte and Charlotte had two more than Abigail.

a) Write an expression for the total number of sweets eaten, in terms of s, where s is the number of sweets eaten by Abigail.

b) If they ate 13 sweets altogether, how many did each person eat?

/2

/40

PAPER 18

1. Here is a pattern called Pascal's triangle.

```
    1  1
   1  2  1
  1  3  3  1
 1  4  6  4  1
```

a) On a separate piece of paper continue the pattern for three more lines.

b) Calculate the sum of the numbers in each line. What do you notice?

_____

c) Circle the sequence of triangular numbers in your pattern.

/3

2. It takes 6 escaped goats 3 hours to eat everything on Mrs Smith's vegetable plot.

a) If all the goats eat at the same rate, how long would it take one goat to clear the same plot?

_____

b) If there were 12 goats how long would it take? _____

/2

3. Janet and John both travel from the same village to a tennis tournament. Janet is taken by car and the journey takes 2 hours travelling at 33 mph. John goes by bus and the journey takes 3 hours. What is the average speed of the bus?

_____

/1

4. Sunni has collected this data on the download times of the music tracks that he buys.

download time t (seconds)	frequency f
$0 < t \leq 20$	2
$20 < t \leq 40$	4
$40 < t \leq 60$	7
$60 < t \leq 80$	12
$80 < t \leq 100$	15
$100 < t \leq 120$	5

a) On a separate piece of graph paper draw a frequency polygon to show this data.

b) Use the data to calculate an estimate of the mean download time.

_____

/4

5. a) Lizzie buys k oranges and w bunches of flowers. If oranges cost 31p each and flowers cost £1.50 a bunch write a formula for the total cost, C, of Lizzie's shopping.

_____

b) If she buys seven times as many oranges as bunches of flowers, and she spends £7.34, how many oranges did she buy?

/3

_____

6. a) Complete this table and, on a separate sheet of graph paper, draw the graph of $y = x^2 - 4$

x	-3	-2	-1	0	1	2	3	4
$y = x^2 - 4$		0			-3			12

b) Use your graph to find the solutions to the equation $x^2 - 4 = 6$

/5

_____

7. On a separate sheet of paper draw the plan, front elevation and side elevation of this shape.

/3

8. The equation $x^3 + x^2 = 27$ has a solution between 2 and 3. Use trial and improvement to find the value of x, correct to 1 decimal place.

/2

_____

9. Write the answers to these calculations.

a) $24 \div (6 + 2) + 5 - 4 + (5 + 2)^2$ _____

b) $\dfrac{4 \times -3 + 24 \div 3}{8}$ _____

c) $7 + 3 \times 4^2 \div (3 + 7)$ _____

/3

10. Here is a graph showing Tammy's journey to school.

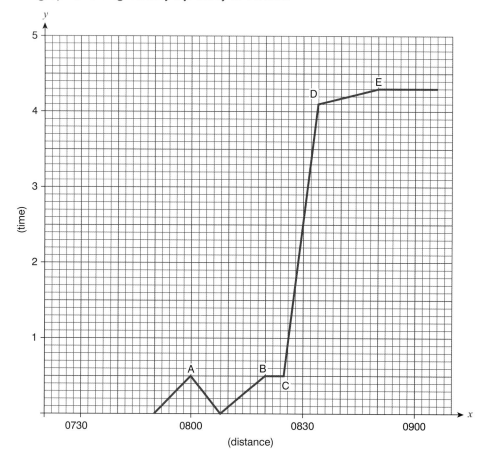

(time)

(distance)

a) What time does she leave for school? _____

b) How far is it to school? _____

c) School registration is at 08.45. Is she late?

_____

d) Part of her journey is by bus. Which part of the graph shows this?

_____

e) What do you think happened between A and B?

/5

_____

11. On a separate sheet of graph paper draw the triangle with vertices at (1, 2), (5, 2) and (4, 4). Using a centre (0, 0):

a) enlarge the triangle with a scale factor of 2

b) enlarge the triangle with a scale factor of $\frac{1}{2}$

/3

12. There are three queues at the supermarket checkouts. There are twice as many people in queue A as in queue B and there are 8 people in queue C.

a) Write an expression for the total number of people queuing.

_____

b) If there are 26 people queuing altogether which queue should you join?

/3

_____

13. A rainwater gutter on a roof has a semi-circular cross section with a radius 6 cm and is 8 m long. When it rains hard the gutter fills up to the brim.

a) Calculate the volume of water in this length of gutter.

_____

b) One cubic metre of water has a mass of 1 tonne (1000 kg).
   What mass of water is there in the rainwater gutter when it is full?

_____

c) The water runs into a 180 litre water butt at a rate of 1600 cm³/minute. How long will it take to fill?

/3

_____

/40

area	the amount of space inside a 2-D shape
arrowhead	a quadrilateral which has one inside angle greater than 180° and one line of symmetry
ascending order	listed from smallest to largest
circumference	the distance around the edge of a circle
correlation	a measure of the strength of relationship between two sets of data – how close they are to forming a straight-line graph
cylinder	a 3-D shape with two identical circular or oval ends joined by one curved side
diameter	the distance from one side of a circle to another which passes through the centre
frequency polygon	a graph made from a frequency histogram by joining the tops of the columns together from the middles
frequency table/chart	a table for a set of observations showing how frequently each event or quantity occurs
intersect	cross over, for example these three lines intersect at P
isosceles trapezium	a trapezium which has both non-parallel sides the same length
kite	a 2-D shape which has two equal pairs of sides which meet each other and equal angles where the pairs meet
mean	the average of a set of numbers calculated by adding the numbers then dividing by how many numbers there are
median	the middle number in a set of numbers which are arranged according to size, the median of 1 3 6 7 9 is 6, the median of 2 4 6 10 is 5 $((4 + 6) \div 2)$
mode	an average which is the number that occurs most often in a set of numbers
net	a 2-D shape that can be cut around and folded to make a 3-D shape, for example, one net for a cube is:
octagon	an eight sided polygon
parallel	two lines are parallel if they are the same distance apart all along their length and never touch or intersect
parallelogram	a four sided shape which has opposite sides parallel and of the same length and with equal opposite angles (this includes squares, rectangles and rhombuses)

pentagon	a five sided polygon (2-D shape)
perimeter	the distance around the edges of a 2-D shape
pie chart	a circular chart divided into sectors representing relative amounts
polygon	a 2-D shape
prime number	a number which can only be divided by 1 and itself without a remainder. 2, 3, 5, 7, 11, and 13 are all prime numbers.
prism	a 3-D shape with two identical sides joined by a number of flat sides
probability	how likely it is that something will happen
quadrilateral	a 2-D shape with 4 sides
radius	the distance between any point on a circle's edge and its centre point
range	the difference between the highest and lowest values of a set of data
ratio	a ratio shows the relative sizes of two or more values separated by ':' For example, the ratio of gold to silver in a coin is 2 : 7
rhombus	a four-sided shape with all sides of equal length
scatter graph	a graph of plotted points that show the relationship between two sets of data
similar	two shapes are similar if they differ only in size and/or orientation, i.e. they must have the same angles and sides in the same ratio
surface area	the sum of the areas of each 2-D face of a 3-D shape
tesselate	form a pattern like a mosaic of shapes repeated without gaps
translation	moving a shape to a different position but keeping the same line lengths and angle values
trapezium	a quadrilateral with just one pair of parallel sides
variable	a letter that represents a value in algebra
vertex/vertices	a point where two or more straight lines meet (a corner). These lettered points are vertices.
volume	the amount of space a 3-D shape fills

Progress grid

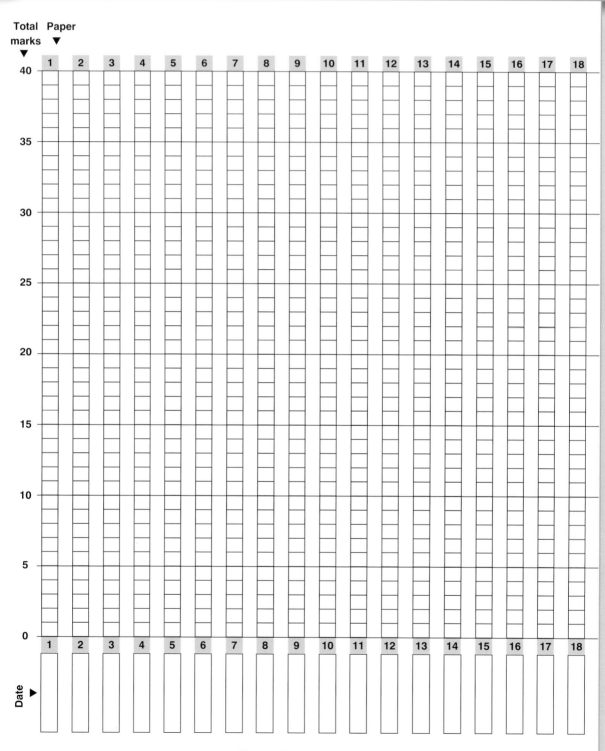

Total marks ▼

Paper ▼

Date ▶

Now colour in your score!

Answer booklet: KS3 Maths Levels 6–7

Paper 1

1. (1, 2)   (1, 5)   (4, 8) *(1 mark each)*
2. Cheap cheep by £10.87 *(1 mark each)*
3. C   D   B   F   E   A *(1 mark)*
4. a) $3x = 20 + 2x - 2$ or equivalent
   b) 16 and 18 *(1 mark each)*
5. 89.28 *(2 marks: 1 for 8928 or 44.64)*
6. $a = 108°$
   $b = 72°$
   $c = 36°$ *(1 mark each)*
7. a)

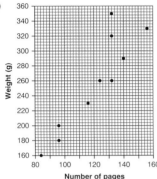

   Weight (g) vs Number of pages

   b) Positive correlation between number of pages
   and weight of a book. *(1 mark each)*
8. 6.975 or 7.0 cm² *(1 mark for number, 1 for units)*
9. a) Enlargement, scale factor 3, centre of enlargement (1, 7)
   (2 marks)
   b) Angles or shape, orientation, or ratio of sides *(1 mark)*
   c)

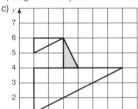

   d) length (size), angle (shape), area *(1 mark)*
10. 0.07 *(1 mark)*
11. a)

Black	✓	✓	✗	✗
White	✓	✗	✓	✗

   Or similar showing 4 different outcomes
   b) ½ *(1 mark each)*
12. A   C   D *(1 mark)*
13. a) 430
   b) 80
   c) 60 *(1 mark each)*
14. a) 94   190 *(1 mark)*
   b) 3   8 *(1 mark each)*
15. $a = 88°$ → opposite angles
   $b = 46°$ → 180° in a triangle
   $c = 46°$ → alternate angles *(1 mark each)*
16. $(5 \times 180 - 360) = 540°$ *(1 mark)*
17. 20   (giving 120 : 40 = 3 : 1) *(1 mark)*
18. a) $\frac{3}{5} + \frac{1}{5} = \frac{28}{25}$
   b) $\frac{4}{5} - \frac{1}{4} = \frac{11}{20}$
   c) $3 \times \frac{2}{9} = \frac{2}{3}$ *(1 mark each)*

Paper 2

1. a) 106° b) 88° *(1 mark each)*
2. a) 20 (cm) b) $6n + 2$ *(1 mark each)*
3. 3 colours (opposite faces have the same colour) *(1 mark)*
4.

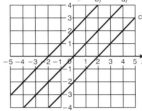

   a) Line $y = x$ drawn
   b) Line $y = x + 2$ drawn
   c) $y = x - 2$ *(1 mark each)*
5. 1.3 m² *(1 mark)*
6. £2.22 *(2 marks: 1 for £1.57 or £2.63)*
7. a)

	Old cream	New cream	Total
Cured	600	450	1050
Not cured	200	150	350
Total	800	600	1400

   b) 1400
   c) 450
   d) (i) 75%
   (ii) 75%
   (iii) both/neither because same % cured in each case.
   (6 marks:1 mark each)
8. 14 *(1 mark)*
9. a) $x = 2$ b) $x = 1$ c) $x = 3$ *(1 mark each)*
10. a)

	Square spinner			
Triangular spinner	1	2	3	4
1	2	3	4	5
2	3	4	5	6
3	4	5	6	7

   b) 6 (2,3,4,5,6,7)
   c) $\frac{11}{12}$ *(1 mark each)*
11. a) 210 cm² b) 231 cm² *(1 mark each)*
12. Odd numbers *(1 mark)*
13. a) £8 b) £96 *(1 mark each)*
14. a) 160 ml
   b) 375 ml (vinegar) 625 ml (olive oil) *(1 mark each)*
15. a) Reflection in the y-axis
   b) 90° clock-wise rotation about (1, 1) or 270° anti-clockwise
   rotation about (1, 1)
   c) 2 to the right and 3 down or 3 down and 2 to the right
   (1 mark each)
16. $\frac{3}{5}$ or $\frac{6}{10}$ *(1 mark)*
17.

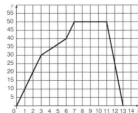

   1 mark for first three lines correct, 1 for last two lines correct

18. In any order:

a) $1 \times 1 \times 24$ $1 \times 2 \times 12$
    $2 \times 2 \times 6$ $2 \times 3 \times 4$ *(1 mark for four or five*
    $3 \times 1 \times 8$ $4 \times 6 \times 1$ *correct)*

b) $2 \times 2 \times 6$ *(2 marks)*

Paper 3

1. a) $\frac{5}{8}$ b) 25%   *(1 mark each)*

2. a) $9n - 4$ b) $n + 3$

   c) $3n$ *(1 mark each)*

3. a) 4   b) -13 *(1 mark each)*

4. $a = 70°$ $b = 35°$ $c = 55°$ *(1 mark each)*

5. a) 0.375   b) 25   *(1 mark each)*

6.

Weight(w kg)	Frequency
$110 \le w < 120$	6
$120 \le w < 130$	5
$130 \le w < 140$	6
$140 \le w < 150$	3

(1 mark each)

7. a) 707 m²   *(1 mark for number,*
                              1 for units)

   b) £56550   *(2 marks: 1 for 56548)*

8. $a = 55°$ $b = 125°$
   $c = 55°$ $d = 125°$ *(1 mark each)*

9. a) $\frac{9}{14}$

   b) $\frac{1}{12}$

   c) $\frac{13}{12}$ or $1\frac{1}{12}$ *(1 mark each)*

10. a) $6x^2 = x^3$

   b) 6 (cm)   *(1 mark each)*

11. $p - 116°$ $q = 40°$ $r = 72°$ *(1 mark each)*

12. 28.5   *(2 marks: 1 for 28.53)*

13. a) negative
   b) no
   c) negative   *(1 mark each)*

14. a) $\frac{1}{6}$

   b) $\frac{2}{6}$ or $\frac{1}{3}$

   c) $\frac{3}{6}$ or $\frac{1}{2}$ *(1 mark each)*

Paper 4

1. a) $x = 8$ b) $x = 7$
   c) $x = 11$ d) $x = 4$ *(1 mark each)*

2.

$\frac{3}{4}$	$\frac{1}{8}$	$\frac{5}{8}$
$\frac{3}{8}$	$\frac{1}{2}$	$\frac{5}{8}$
$\frac{3}{8}$	$\frac{7}{8}$	$\frac{1}{4}$

(1 mark each)

3. $a = 50°$ because alternate angle
   $b = 130°$ because 180° in a straight line
   $c = 95°$ because 360° in quadrilateral   *(1 mark each)*

4. a) 33 $(= 12 + 10 + 7 + 3 + 1)$
   b) 8
   c) Malster because they have more apples that are heavier.
                                       (1 mark each)

5. a)

	Number on the other dice						
Number on one dice		**1**	**2**	**3**	**4**	**5**	**6**
	1	0	1	2	3	4	5
	2	1	0	1	2	3	4
	3	2	1	0	1	2	3
	4	3	2	1	0	1	2
	5	4	3	2	1	0	1
	6	5	4	3	2	1	0

b) $\frac{18}{36}$ or $\frac{1}{2}$
c) No because Jennifer has a higher
   probability of winning   *(1 mark each)*

6. a) £2   b) 90 kg   *(1 mark each)*

7. 35%   *(1 mark)*

8. a) $\frac{42}{50} = 84\%$
   b) Copper is 162 g   c) 81%   *(1 mark each)*

9. Between 6 m and 7 m   *(1 mark)*

10. a) 75%   b) $84 : 16 = 21 : 4$ *(1 mark each)*

11. a) $g = 3w + 2$ b) 362   *(1 mark each)*

12. 1 = A   2 = B   3 = A
   4 = A   5 = B   6 = B   *(2 marks: 1 i*
                                one error)

13. Any three of these (in any order):
   $36 \times 1 \times 1$ $18 \times 2 \times 1$ $2 \times 2 \times 9$
   $3 \times 4 \times 3$ $6 \times 6 \times 1$ $2 \times 3 \times 6$
   $9 \times 4 \times 1$ *(1 mark)*

14.

Start & Finish

(1 mark)

15. a) (314 to 314.2) metres (depending on π value)
   b) (3.1 to 3.8) times round
   c) (7750 to 7854) m²   *(1 mark each)*

16. a) 67% → 241°   16% → 58°   *(1 mark)*
   b) Correct pie chart, angles accurate $\pm2°$, labelled   *(1 mark)*

■ 0 to 14 □ 15 to 64 ▨ 65+

17. a) = [5]   b) = [2]   c) = [1]   d) = [8]   *(1 mark each)*

Paper 5

1. a)

		Score on dice						
		1	**2**	**3**	**4**	**5**	**6**
Coin	Head (H)	H1	**H2**	**H3**	**H4**	**H5**	**H6**
	Tail (T)	**T1**	**T2**	**T3**	**T4**	**T5**	**T6**

b) $\frac{1}{12}$ c) $\frac{3}{12}$ or $\frac{1}{4}$ *(1 mark each)*

2. 0.18 m³ or 180000 cm³   *(1 mark for number, 1 for units)*

3. $x = 30°$ *(1 mark)*

4. (13.07 to 13.26) metres depending on value for π used   *(1 mark)*

5. 0.9815 (1 − 0.0185)   *(1 mark)*

6. a) $4x + 3 = 23$ or $4x = 20$ *(1 mark)*
   b) 8 cm   4 cm   11 cm   *(2 marks: 1 for two correct)*

7. a)

Height	Frequency
100 to 109	2
110 to 119	7
120 to 129	11
130 to 139	9
140 to 149	3
150 to 159	1

(2 marks: 1 if two errors)

b) 20 children   *(1 mark)*

8. 15.7   *(2 marks: 1 for 15 to 16)*

9.

      a)   b)   c)

(1 mark each)

10.

Quadrilateral	Diagonals always cut at right angles	Number of lines of symmetry	Order of rotation symmetry
Rectangle	No	2	2
Square	**Yes**	4	4
Kite	Yes	1	0
Parallelogram	No	0	2
Rhombus	Yes	2	2

(4 marks: 3 for 9 or 10 correct, 2 for 7 or 8 correct and 1 for 5 or 6 correct)

11. $\frac{3}{4}, \frac{1}{8}$ and $\frac{1}{2}, \frac{3}{8}$ *(1 mark)*

12. No because it shows positive correlation *(1 mark)*

13. 0.015   5%   15% $\frac{1}{5}$ 0.5 $\frac{15}{20}$ *(1 mark)*

14. a) 46% b) 45%
c) 47% *(1 mark each)*

15. a) 17 b) 32
c) $3n + 2$ *(1 mark each)*

16. $y = 6 - x$ *(1 mark)*

17. 5% *(1 mark)*

18. Copper: 252° Nickel: 20°
Zinc: 88° *(2 marks: 1 if two correct)*

19. FD1 RT90 FD2 **RT270** FD1 **RT270** FD4 **RT270** FD2
(accept LT90 or RT270) *(2 marks: 1 if first three correct)*

20. $a + 10b$ *(1 mark)*

21. 72 seconds *(1 mark)*

Paper 6

1. a) 3, 8, 13 *(1 mark)*
b) 21 *(2 marks: 1 for 20)*

2. 25.7 *(2 marks: 1 for 25)*

3. $a = 115°$ $b = 65°$
$c = 25°$ $d = 90°$ *(1 mark each)*

4. a) 40 cm² *(2 marks each: 1 for*
b) 16 cm³ *number, 1 for unit)*

5. a) $x = 27$
b) $x = 8$
c) $x = -3$ *(1 mark each)*

6. a) true
b) false
c) true *(1 mark each)*

7. a) $\frac{4}{45}$
b) 48
c) 3 or 3.1 or 3.06 *(1 mark each)*

8. $a = 134°$ $b = 46°$ $c = 134°$ *(1 mark each)*

9. a) 10.6
b) 9.42 *(1 mark each)*

10. a) C b) B
c) A d) B *(1 mark each)*

11. a)

Number	1	2	3	4	5	6
Probability	$\frac{1}{6}$	$\frac{1}{6}$	$\frac{1}{6}$	$\frac{1}{6}$	$\frac{1}{6}$	$\frac{1}{6}$

(1 mark)

b)

Number	1	2	3	4	5	6
Probability	$\frac{1}{9}$	$\frac{1}{6}$	$\frac{1}{6}$	$\frac{1}{6}$	$\frac{1}{6}$	$\frac{2}{9}$

(1 mark for the $\frac{1}{6s}$, 1 for $\frac{1}{9}$ and 1 for $\frac{2}{9}$)

12. a) 28
b) 16 *(1 mark each)*

13. a) 78.5 *(1 mark)*
b) 21.5 *(2 marks: 1 for 21 to 22)*

Paper 7

1. a) $x = 20°$ because the angles are alternate angles (or similar)
b) $y + 20 = 40$ because the angles are alternate angles (or similar) so $y = 20°$
c) isosceles *(1 mark each)*

2. a) 36 *(1 mark)*
b) 300 cm² *(2 marks)*

3. $8\frac{3}{4}$ *(1 mark)*

4. *(2 marks)*

a	5	6	27	35
b	12.5	15	67.5	87.5

---

5. a) square, kite, rectangle, rhombus, parallelogram, trapezium
b) square, rectangle
c) square, rhombus, kite *(1 mark each)*

6. a) (i) $3x$ (ii) $4x$ *(1 mark each)*
b) false true
true true *(2 marks: 1 for three correct)*

7. DEF (1 : 2) AC (2 : 3) BGH (3 : 2) *(2 marks: 1 for at least one correct)*

8. a) 30 b) 1 c) 3 *(1 mark each)*

9. $\frac{4}{24}$ $\frac{1}{4}$ $\frac{15}{48}$ $\frac{7}{12}$ $\frac{9}{12}$ $\frac{19}{24}$ *(1 mark)*

10. a)

Price of bottle of water (£) vs Distance from city centre (km)

(2 marks: 1 for eight or nine points plotted correctly)

b) Yes, there is negative correlation *(1 mark)*

11. 9 *(1 mark)*

12. a) $\frac{47}{60}$ b) $\frac{4}{5}$
c) 6 d) $\frac{3}{5}$ *(1 mark each)*

13. a) 60
b) 150 *(1 mark each)*

14.

A   B   C *(1 mark each)*

15. a) 6 b) 24 *(1 mark each)*

16.

◇	A	B	C	D	E	F	G	H	I
1	3	1	4	5	9	14	23	37	60
2	3	6	12	24	48	96	192	384	768
3	3	1	−1	−3	−5	−7	−9	−11	−13

(3 marks: 1 for each correct row)

Paper 8

1. a) $\frac{31}{24}$ or $\frac{17}{24}$ b) $\frac{17}{20}$ *(1 mark each)*

2. 0.069, 0.6, 0.609, 0.61, 0.629, 0.631, 0.692 *(1 mark)*

3. a) $C = 2d + 4a$
b) $500 - (2d + 4a)$ or $500 - 2d - 4a$ *(1 mark each)*

4. $a = 92°$, $b = 88°$, $c = 40°$,
$d = 40°$, $e = 40°$, $f = 38°$, *(4 marks: ½*
$g = 44°$, $h = 98°$ *for each and round down)*

5. a) 12 b) 75 c) 12 *(1 mark each)*

6. a) 4:10:9:3 *(2 marks: 1 for three correct)*
b) 6:7 *(1 mark)*

7. 90°, 37°, 53° (all ±2°) *(1 mark)*

8. a) 56 b) 44.24
c) 442.4 *(1 mark each)*

9. Must have tally and frequency columns and cover all possible destination options. e.g.

Destination	Tally	Frequency
England		
Scotland		
France		
America		
Other		
stayed at home		

(2 marks: 1 for one error)

10. a) $\frac{n}{4} - 2 = 5$, $n = 28$ *(1 mark)*
b) $3b = b + 90$ $b = 45$ or 45p a banana *(2 marks)*

11.

under 10, 11–20, 21–30, 31–50, over 50

angles 180°, 40°, 10°, 70°, 60°

(2 marks: 1 if one or two errors)

12. 24 km = 15 miles;
4 km = 2.5 miles;
30 miles = 48 km;
200 miles = 320 km *(½ mark each: round total down)*

13. a) Area ABC = 40 cm²
b) volume = 400 cm³ *(1 mark each)*

14.

coin\dice	1	2	3	4	5	6
H	H1	H2	H3	H4	H5	H6
T	T1	T2	T3	T4	T5	T6

a) $\frac{2}{12} = \frac{1}{6}$
b) $\frac{3}{12} = \frac{1}{4}$
c) no the game is not fair. (Eric is more likely to win) *(1 mark each)*

15.

	2 pairs of parallel sides	1 or 0 pairs of parallel sides
equal length diagonals	square, rectangle	isosceles trapezium
unequal diagonals	rhombus, parallelogram	kite, trapezium

(1 mark for each correct cell: maximum of 3)

16. 3.33 kg *(1 mark)*

17. a) 5
b) 10 *(1 mark each)*

Paper 9

1. $\frac{1}{2}$ $\frac{3}{4}$ $\frac{7}{8}$ $\frac{9}{10}$ $\frac{19}{20}$ *(1 mark)*

2. a) £108   60%
b) 40% *(1 mark each)*

3. a) 29.1
b) 32
c) mean is affected by the one very low mark, so median probably the better. *(1 mark each)*

4.

(2 marks: 1 for three or four correct)

5. a) 6 : 5
b) £15 *(1 mark each)*

6. a) 2 × (3² + 5) × 4 = 112
b) 2 × 3² + 5 × 4 = 38
c) (2 × 3)² + 5 × 4 = 56 *(1 mark each)*

7. a) 136 °F
b) −67 °C *(1 mark each)*

8. a) 1.13 m²
b) 11310 cm² *(1 mark each)*

9. a) It is a leading question.
For example: Do you think exercise is necessary for a healthy life style? With response boxes: Yes No Don't know
b) Most people outside a sports centre will already do sports. A weekday morning will give a very limited sample of people. *(1 mark each)*

10.

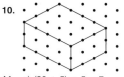

(1 mark)

11. a) (30 + 5) ÷ 5 = 7
b) 7.5625
c) 7.6 *(1 mark each)*

12.

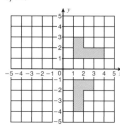

(1 mark)

13. a) 23   2n + 3
b) 49   3n + 19 *(2 marks each)*

14.

	equal sides	number of axes of symmetry	order of rotational symmetry
square	all 4 equals	4	4
rectangle	2 pairs	2	2
Parallelogram	2 pairs	0	2
trapezium	none	0	none
isosceles trapezium	1 pair	1	none
kites	2 pairs	1	none
rhombus	all 4 equals	2	2
arrowhead (delta)	2 pairs	1	none

(3 marks: 1 for each correct column in table)

15. 2.4 m = 240 cm = 2400 mm
3.8 km = 3800 m = 380000 cm
79 mm = 7.9 cm
5.3 kg = 5300 g
3 cm² = 300 mm² *(2 marks: ½ for each correct row then round down)*

16. a) C   b) A   c) B *(2 marks: 1 for two correct)*

17. a) 6.25 (accept answers 6.2 − 6.3)
b) −2.8 and +2.8 (accept answers 2.7 − 2.9) *(1 mark each)*

18.

	adults	children	total
on foot	15	8	23
bike	4	6	10
horse	5	4	9
pedal car	0	1	1
motor-bike	11	0	11
total	35	19	54

a) Walking
b) $\frac{23}{54}$ *(1 mark each)*

Paper 10

1. $\frac{29}{61}$ 0.492 $\frac{5}{9}$ $\frac{7}{11}$ $\frac{9}{13}$ *(1 mark)*

2. 9.2 *(1 mark)*

3. a) x = 10   b) x = 9.5 *(1 mark each)*

4. a) 24 × 25000 = 600000 miles *(1 mark)*
b) 60 days or 1440 hours *(2 marks: 1 for 120 days)*

5. 25 × 50 = 1250
10 ÷ 0.05 = 200
25 × 0.05 = 1.25
0.05 ÷ 10 = 0.005
50 ÷ 0.05 = 1000 *(3 marks: 2 for four correct, 1 for three)*

6. 21% *(1 mark)*

7. a) 4x + 6 < 100, x < 23.5
b) 23   24   25   26 *(1 mark each)*

8. a)

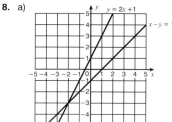

(2 marks: 1 for each correctly drawn straight line)

b) x = −2, y = −3 *(1 mark)*

9. 10.05 seconds to 10.15 seconds *(1 mark)*

10. a) 36 equally likely outcomes:

	2	3	4	4	5	6
1	1, 2	1, 3	1, 4	1, 4	1, 5	1, 6
2	2, 2	2, 3	2, 4	2, 4	2, 5	2, 6
3	3, 2	3, 3	3, 4	3, 4	3, 5	3, 6
3	3, 2	3, 3	3, 4	3, 4	3, 5	3, 6
4	4, 2	4, 3	4, 4	4, 4	4, 5	4, 6
5	5, 2	5, 3	5, 4	5, 4	5, 5	5, 6

b) $\frac{2}{36}$ or $\frac{1}{18}$
c) 7 (8 ways it may occur) *(1 mark each)*

11. a) 52.5
   b) 100 mm or 120 mm
   c) $60 < r \leqslant 80$ *(1 mark each)*
12. 5000 cm²
   or 0.5 m² *(1 mark for number, 1 for units)*
13. a) enlargement scale factor $\frac{1}{2}$ centre (5, 3) *(2 marks)*
   b) Angle *(1 mark)*
14. 1 3 6 10
   4 8 9
   2 5 7 *(2 marks: 1 for one or two correct)*
15. a) 20   b) $n(n + 1)$
   c) 4   6   8 *(1 mark each)*
16.

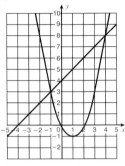

   a) Smooth curve of above general shape
   b) Correctly drawn straight line
   c) $(-1, 3)$ $(4, 8)$ *(1 mark each)*
17. $A = (96 - 100)°$ $B = (50 - 54)°$ *(1 mark each)*
18. a) $x^2 + 4x + 4$ b) $x^2 + x - 6$ *(1 mark each)*

Paper 11
1. $a = 3, b = 7$ *(1 mark each)*
2.

   (1 mark)
3. a) 54 cm²   b) 18 cm³ *(1 mark each)*
4. $x = 5$ *(1 mark)*
5. 4, 5, 6 and 7 *(1 mark)*
6. a) 138   b) 17 or 16.6 (...) *(1 mark each)*
7. a) $x^2 - 4x - 5$ b) $x^2 + 4x + 4$ *(1 mark each)*
8. Mean or median is 3.5 Mode is 4 *(1 mark each)*
9. a) (6.5 to 7.5) km   b) (18 to 20) km *(1 mark each)*
10. a) 2.3 steps per second
   b) Taipei 101
   2.37 steps per second *(1 mark each)*
11. a) $1\frac{1}{8}$ or $\frac{9}{8}$
   b) $2\frac{1}{2}$ or $\frac{5}{2}$
   c) $\frac{2}{3}$ *(1 mark each)*
12. a) 1
   b) $\frac{11}{50}$
   c) $\frac{46}{50}$ or $\frac{23}{25}$ *(1 mark each)*
13. 3.85 *(1 mark)*
14.

Red	1	1	1	2	2	3	3	4	4	5	6
Blue	1	2	3	1	2	1	2	1	2	1	1

(1 mark)
15. a) $1 + \sqrt{9} = \sqrt{16}$
   b) $\sqrt{16} + \sqrt{4} = \sqrt{36}$ *(1 mark each)*
16. Larger by 3.6 cm² *(1 mark each)*
17. a) 50
   b) 5 *(1 mark each)*
18. $a = 4w - b - c - d$ *(1 mark)*
19. On $(1,1)$ $(0, -1)$
   Above $(0, 0)$, $(-1, 0)$
   Below $(2, 4)$, $(4, 5)$ *(2 marks: 1 for one correct)*

20. a)

Cost C (£)	Frequency
$60 \leq C < 70$	1
$70 \leq C < 80$	3
$80 \leq C < 90$	6
$90 \leq C < 100$	4
$100 \leq C < 110$	10
$110 \leq C < 120$	3
$120 \leq C < 130$	3

(1 mark)
   b)

(2 marks: or 1 for at least six points correctly plotted, 1 for closed polygon.)
21. 128 newtons *(1 mark)*
22. B D H E
   F G K
   A I J *(1 mark)*

Paper 12
1. 2 cm   3 cm   4 cm *(1 mark)*
   24 cm³ *(1 mark for number, 1 for units)*
2. a) Between 20.5 °C and 21.5 °C
   b) Between 25 °C and 27 °C *(1 mark each)*
3.

(2 marks: 1 for correctly scaled drawing on square and attempt to draw at least one arc)
4. a) 500 m³ *(1 mark for number, 1 for units)*
   b) 625 minutes or 10 hours 25 minutes *(1 mark for number, 1 for units)*
   c) 500 tonnes *(1 mark)*
5. 402200 *(1 mark)*
6. 36 or 36.05 or 36.1 ... cm *(1 mark)*
7. a) $\frac{5}{98}$
   b) Carry with more trials (increase the number of trials) *(1 mark each)*
8. $a = \frac{y - b}{x}$ *(1 mark)*
9. All % to nearest whole number.
   a) 70%
   b) Probably not, 60%   74% *(1 mark each)*
10. $a < c$ $b < c$
   Cannot be certain $a < c$ *(2 marks: 1 for three correct)*
11. a) $\frac{15.176 \times 0913}{102.8 \times 0.0311} \approx \frac{15 \times 1}{100 \times 0.03} = 5$
   b) $\frac{\sqrt{17} \times 3.1}{1.97 \times 2.1} \approx \frac{4 \times 3}{2 \times 2} = 3$ *(1 mark each)*
12. a) $1\frac{7}{8}$ $2\frac{1}{4}$ $2\frac{5}{8}$ 3 $3\frac{3}{8}$
   b) $8\frac{8}{9}$ $8\frac{1}{3}$ $7\frac{7}{9}$ $7\frac{2}{9}$ $6\frac{2}{3}$ *(1 mark each)*
13. 6 and 7 *(1 mark)*
14. 62.5 minutes *(1 mark)*
15. a)

Temperature T (°C)	Tally	Frequency
$10 \leq T < 15$		0
$15 \leq T < 20$	///	3
$20 \leq T < 25$	###	5
$25 \leq T < 30$	### ///	8
$30 \leq T < 35$	////	4
$35 \leq T < 40$		0

(1 mark)

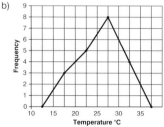

b)

(2 marks: 1 for 5 or more points correctly plotted, 1 for closed polygon)

c) (i) Mean temperature = 24.95 °C

(ii) Estimated mean temperature = 25.75 °C   *(1 mark each)*

(1 mark)

16. $\frac{3}{16}$

17. a)

x	0	1	2	3	4	5	6
y	0	12	12	6	0	0	12

(2 marks: 1 for two or three correct)

b)   *(2 marks: 1 for at least six points plotted correctly, 1 for smooth curve passing sensibly through all points)*

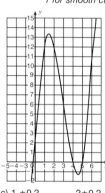

c) 1 ±0.2   2±0.2   6±0.2   *(2 marks: 1 for two correct)*

Paper 13

1. The answer is always 1.   *(1 mark)*

2. (92.5 by 56.5) to (93.5 by 57.5) giving 5226.25 to 5376.25 or 5226 to 5376   *(1 mark)*

3. a) $10 < 2x$ or $2x > 10$ giving solution $x > 5$

b) $7 + x > 0$, giving $x > -7$ *(1 mark each)*

4. a)   *(1 mark)*

Both the inner and outer circle are needed.

b) 74.4 cm²   *(1 mark for number, 1 for units)*

5. Approximate coverage A cm² is given by $(0.1 \div 100) \times A = 5000$, giving an area of 500 m²

So not very reasonable (a very large proportion is lost by evaporation)   *(1 mark)*

6. a) 5   12   13   *(2 marks: 1 for one or two correct groupings)*

b) 7   24   25

c) 8   15   17

7. £226.62 or £226.63   *(1 mark)*

8. 3, 5, and 9   *(2 marks: 1 for two correct)*

9. 32 or 30 cm³   *(1 mark)*

10. a) $a = \frac{2V}{bc}$

b) 12.5   *(1 mark each)*

11. a) $\frac{38}{52}$ or $\frac{19}{26}$

b) About 5, 6 or 7 times (any one is sufficient)   *(1 mark each)*

12.

×	$\frac{3}{4}$	$\frac{4}{7}$	$\frac{8}{9}$	$\frac{1}{2}$
$1\frac{1}{2}$	$1\frac{1}{8}$	$\frac{6}{7}$	$1\frac{1}{3}$	$\frac{3}{4}$
$\frac{3}{4}$	$\frac{9}{16}$	$\frac{3}{7}$	$\frac{2}{3}$	$\frac{3}{8}$
$\frac{7}{8}$	$\frac{21}{32}$	$\frac{1}{2}$	$\frac{7}{9}$	$\frac{7}{16}$

(4 marks: 1 for each correct cell)

13. -1, 0 and 1 (allow just -1 and 1)   *(1 mark)*

14. The following points are on the curve: *(1 mark)*
(0, 0), (4, 4) and (5, 25)

15. 1398.0   *(1 mark)*

16. a) 62 or 63 m (depending on value used for π)

b) 6 m²   *(1 mark each)*

17. a) $\frac{\sqrt{17.01}}{\sqrt{3.9} \times \sqrt{4.1}} \approx \frac{4}{2 \times 2} = 1$

b) $\frac{195^3}{\sqrt{625}} \approx \frac{8}{8} = 1$

c) $2\sqrt{80} + 1.97^2 \approx 18 + 4 = 22$
(allow an answer of 20)   *(1 mark each)*

18. Group 1 $(x + 2)(x + 2)$, $x^2 + 4x + 4$
Group 2 $x^2 + 4$, $x(x + 4) + 4(1 - x)$, $(x - 1)(x + 1) + 5$
Group 3 $(x + 2)(x - 6) + 12$, $x(x - 4)$, $x^2 - 4x$ *(2 marks: 1 for one or two correct groupings)*

19. $(4, -1)$ *(2 marks: 1 for each correct coordinate)*

20. a) 30 and 42

b) $n(n + 1)$ or $n^2 + n$ *(1 mark each)*

21. [A] → 5   [B] → 4
[C] → 7   [D] → 2   *(2 marks: 1 for three correct)*

22. One or more of these:

Side of square	Area	Perimeter	squared
1	1	4	16
2	4	8	64
3	9	12	144

(1 mark)

Perimeter squared is 16 x area or equivalent   *(1 mark)*
(or $(4x)^2 = 16 x^2$. Area of square $= x^2$)   *(1 mark each)*

Paper 14

1. a) £178.60   *(2 marks: 1 for £94)*

b) £24.31   *(2 marks: 1 for £23.15)*

2. a) 27   b) 32   *(1 mark each)*

3. a) Points plotted   *(1 mark)*
Points joined with straight lines   *(1 mark)*
Polygon   *(1 mark)*

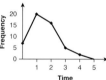

b) 1   *(1 mark)*

4. a) 4   *(2 marks)*
b) 16   *(1 mark)*
c) 16   *(1 mark)*

5. a) no   b) no
c) yes   d) no   *(1 mark each)*

6. a) $x = 16, y = 3$ *(1 mark each)*
b) $x = \frac{1}{2}, y = -2$ *(1 mark each)*

7. 6.30   *(2 marks: 1 for 6.2)*

8. a) ALWAYS   b) SOMETIMES
c) SOMETIMES   d) NEVER
e) SOMETIMES   *(1 mark each)*

9. a) Minimum = 131   Maximum = 144
b) Minimum = 3.62   Maximum = 3.63   *(1 mark each)*

10. a) 72
b) 50
c) 8   *(1 mark each)*

11. a) $\frac{5}{3}$ *(2 marks: 1 for 6:10, $\frac{6}{10}$ or 3:5)*
b) 15   *(1 mark)*
c) 4.5   *(1 mark)*

Paper 15

1. a) 5.69
   b) 2.81 *(1 mark each)*
2. 20 *(1 mark)*
   $\frac{10}{120}$ or $\frac{1}{12}$ or 0.0833 *(1 mark)*
3. a) First column: 5, 20, 45, 90 *(1 mark for each column)*
      Second column: 20, 140, 360, 540
   b) 42.4 *(1 mark)*
   c) $30 \leq x < 60$ *(1 mark)*
   d) 120 *(1 mark)*
4. a) 6000 *(1 mark)*
   b) 0.3 *(1 mark)*
   c) 8 mins 20 seconds *(1 mark each)*
5. a) False   b) True
   c) False   d) True *(1 mark each)*
6. a) A (15,0)   B (0,−6) *(1 mark each)*
   b) (−10,−10) *(1 mark)*
7. a) 19.8 *(2 marks: 1 for answer in range 19 to 20)*
   b) 2 *(1 mark)*
8. a) 60 *(2 marks: 1 for 120)*
   b) 8 *(1 mark)*
9. a) 29.5, 30.5   b) 24599.5, 24600.5
   c) 95, 105   d) 97.5, 102.5 *(1 mark each)*
10. a) Horizontal line drawn from centre of circle
    (2 marks: 1 for correct line, 1 for clarity/presentation)
    b)

    (2 marks: 1 for correct line, 1 for clarity/presentation)
11. a) 4, 13, 28, 49, 76 *(2 marks)*
    b) $n^2 + 4$ 2504 *(2 marks: 1 for each term)*
12. 8 years *(2 marks: 1 for 7 or 9 years as answer)*

Paper 16

1. $\frac{3}{5}$ 0.609   0.64 $\frac{2}{3}$ 69%   73% *(1 mark)*
2. a) $\frac{3}{18} = \frac{1}{6}$
   b) $\frac{4}{18} = \frac{2}{9}$
   c) $\frac{17}{18}$ *(1 mark each)*
3. $x = 81°$ angles on a straight line add up to 180°, angles in a
   quadrilateral add up to 360° *(2 marks)*
   $y = 83°$ angles on a straight line add up to 180° *(2 marks)*
4. a) 4 : 3 : 1 *(2 marks: 1 for 32:24:8)*
   b) $\frac{1}{5}$ *(2 marks: 1 for $\frac{16}{80}$)*
   c) 10% *(1 mark)*
5. TU = 8.4 cm
   PR = 2.8 cm *(1 mark each)*
6. a) 4   b) i) 26   ii) −1 *(1 mark each)*
7. a)
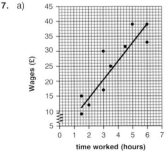
   time worked (hours)
   (2 marks: 1 for correct axes labels, 1 for at least 8 points correctly plotted)
   b) Wages increase as the number of hours
      increases (positive correlation). *(1 mark)*
   c) Line of best fit drawn (see a) above)
      £ (30 − 35) *(1 mark)*
8. Sam is faster; (4.5 km in 20 minutes = 13.5 km/h)
   so by 0.5 km/h *(1 mark each)*

9. a) 30 cm² *(1 mark)*
   b) (i) BC² = AB² + AC² or BC = √169
      (ii) 13 cm *(1 mark each)*
   c) (30 × 2) + (40 + 96 + 104) = 300 cm²
      (2 marks: or 1 for either of the two bracketed expressions seen)
10. a) C = 1.5h + 5   b) £9.50 *(1 mark each)*
11. a)

x	−2	−1	0	1	2
y	0	2	4	6	8

    (2 marks: 1 for four correct cells)
    b) Correctly drawn straight line
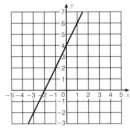
    (2 marks: 1 for straight line through incorrect points)
12. 1.81481481
    1.8 *(1 mark each)*
13. a) 27, 30, 33 *(1 mark)*
    b) 3n + 12 *(1 mark each: 1 for each correct part of the expression)*

Paper 17

1. a) 105 : 15 = 7 : 1
   b) 3.5 h or 3 h 30 min *(1 mark each)*
2. a)
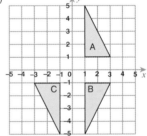
   b) Rotation 180°/half turn about (0,0)/origin *(1 mark each)*
3. a) Diameter 2.8 m
   b) 2.8 m length needed cost £42.00
   c) Ribbon needed 8.80 m cost £39.58 *(1 mark each)*
4. a) $\frac{54.6 \times 27.5}{0.49}$ is about $\frac{50 \times 30}{0.5} = 3000$ *(2 marks)*
   b) 3064.3 *(1 mark)*
5. a) 15%
   b) £289.10 *(1 mark each)*
6. 15.35 s and 15.45 s *(1 mark each)*
7. a) one line of symmetry
   b) e.g.
   (1 mark each)
8. a) 0   b) 126   c) 48 *(2 marks: 1 for just two correct)*
9.

   3 cm
   (2 marks: 1 for two horizontal lines, 1 for two semi-circles)

10. a)

Score	1	2	3	4	5	6
Raoul's	5	6	3	5	8	23
relative frequency	0.10	0.12	0.06	0.10	0.16	0.46
Susan	0	16	5	10	0	19
relative frequency	0	0.32	0.10	0.20	0	0.38

(2 marks: ½ for each correct cell, round down)

b) Susan's spinner is likely to have neither the numbers 1 nor 5
(1 mark)

c) Raoul is most likely to get a 6 first, but cannot be certain
(1 mark)

11. a) $a = 12$ b) $b = 4$ (or -4)
c) $c = 3$ *(1 mark each)*

12. a) 99 103 107
b) $4n + 79$
c) 2, 5, 10, 17 *(1 mark each)*

13. 2.4 m *(2 marks: 1 for 2.449)*

14. a) Questionnaire must include a timeframe e.g. how many hours "per week" "per night" and at least 3 response boxes that do not overlap, e.g. 0 - 1 hour ; 1h 1min - 2 hours, "more than this" *(2 marks)*

b)

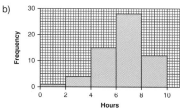

(2 marks: 1 for correct height and width of bars, 1 for labelled axes)

c) Modal class $6 \leqslant h < 8$,
range 10 hours *(1 mark each)*

15. a) $s + (s + 5) + (s + 2) = 3s + 7$
b) Abigail 2, Charlotte 4, Will 7 *(1 mark each)*

Paper 18

1.

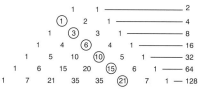

a) 3 correct lines added. *(1 mark)*
b) They are doubling each time or are powers of two. *(1 mark)*
c) All triangular numbers circled *(1 mark)*

2. a) 18 hours,
b) 1.5 hours *(1 mark each)*

3. 22 mph *(1 mark)*

4. a)

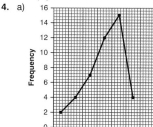

(2 marks: 1 for at least 5 points correctly plotted, 1 for polygon formed)

b) 71.8 seconds *(2 marks: 1 for answer in range 70 to 73 seconds)*

5. a) $C = 0.31k + 1.5w$
or $C = 31k + 150w$ *(2 marks: 1 for each correct term)*
b) 2 bunches of flowers and 14 oranges *(1 mark)*

6. a) Correctly completed table.

x	-3	-2	-1	0	1	2	3	4
$y = x^2 - 4$	5	0	-3	-4	-3	0	5	12

(1 mark)

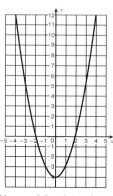

(2 marks: 1 for at least 5 points correctly plotted, 1 for smooth curve)

b) $x = -3.2 \pm 0.1$ and 3.2 ± 0.1 *(1 mark each)*

7.

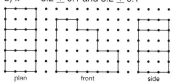

plan   front   side *(1 mark each)*

8. 2.7 *(2 marks: 1 for answer in range 2.6 to 2.8)*

9. a) 53
b) -0.5
c) 11.8 *(1 mark each)*

10. a) 0750
b) 4.3 km
c) yes, she gets to school at 0850
d) between C and D
e) She forgot something and had to go home for it. *(1 mark each)*

11.

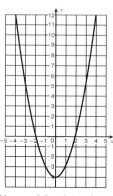

(1 mark each)

12. a) $n + 2n + 8 = 3n + 8$ *(2 marks: 1 for each correct part)*
b) $3n + 8 = 26$, $n = 6$
so join queue B which has 6 people *(1 mark)*

13. a) 45239 cm² or 45.2 litres or 45 litres,
b) 45.2 kg or 45 kg or 0.0452 tonnes
or 0.045 tonnes
c) 112.5 minutes *(1 mark each)*